Cathartic. Quite possibly as healing of an experience for the reader as it must have been for each of the gifted young writers.

—Chris Brown, Interdisciplinary Studies Environmental Program (INSTEP) Co-Founder and Teacher of the Year, Edmonds School District

Unforgettable first-person stories of resilient teens overcoming adversity and transforming their lives. An inspirational and amazing read!

—Dr. Cal Crow, Educator and Lead Trainer for the Center for Efficacy and Resiliency

What a joy to witness these writers free themselves of the past and move on to the bright futures they deserve. They have transformed our school with their courage.

—Kathy Clift, former Scriber Lake High School Principal

D1403284

I'M FINALLY AWAKE

I'M FINALLY
AWAKE

Young Authors Untangling Old Nightmares

Compiled and Edited by Marjie Bowker and David Zwaschka

STEEP STAIRS
PRESS

For information, contact:

Steep Stairs Press
23200 100th Ave. W.
Edmonds, WA 98020
425-431-7270

www.steepstairspress.com

www.facebook.com/steepstairspress

ISBN-13:978-0-9974724-0-0

Library of Congress Control Number: 2016941692

Cover Design by Jose Pulido
www.pulido.co

Print book and eBook formatting by Hydra House
www.hydrahousebooks.com

Editing assistance by Carol Bowker and Shalyn Ensz

There is no greater agony than bearing an untold story inside you.

—Maya Angelou

A NOTE BEFORE YOU READ

As you read these stories, keep in mind that some events may be triggering for someone who has experienced the same trauma. Remember to monitor your emotions—if you find yourself unable to continue, take a break, talk to a trusted individual, or go on to the next story.

TABLE OF CONTENTS

FOREWORD

A Note from Marjie Bowker

I'm Finally Awake—this year's title comes from a class poem created last fall by many of the writers in this collection. Danika Henson ("Plus I Love You") wrote the line, inspired by the Mac Miller song she mentions at the end of her story. We all looked at each other when the poem was complete, knowing that line would be our next book title.

The title speaks to the most important goal of this storytelling program: using the writing process to gain self-awareness—the knowledge that we have the power to be the authors of our own lives.

Another book could be written telling the stories behind each writer's process. Sarah Jean ("Thirteen") and MaKayla Boulet ("Contact High") both began writing theirs as freshmen and are now publishing two and three years later. Shalyn Ensz ("They") and Andrew Ekstedt ("Cough and Cold Sweats") approached me at the beginning of this school year saying they wanted to bring the issues of schizophrenia and addiction to cold medicine, respectively, out in the open. Ali Verzola ("Any Last Words?") felt it was time to face her mother's death—really face it. Kelly Makaveli ("Stepping from Oblivion"), a 2013 graduate, is in the process of writing a book; because she is still a source of inspiration to many students at Scriber since being published in *You've Got it All Wrong*, she was invited to make a cameo appearance here with her first chapter. Each story has a courageous writer behind it who desired to face the past in order to find healing and to help others. To mention that these students inspire me daily is, well, an understatement.

Many people ask about the writing process—how do students' stories end up in the Scriber books? The writing begins during a class narrative writing unit. After completing two drafts, students have the option to move their stories forward toward publication. Each spring our school holds a week-long mini-course where teachers cover a subject of their choice, and Dave Zwaschka and I have taught the publishing mini-course for the past few years. Each day we work on all aspects of the publishing process; it is not unusual for stories to go through seven to fifteen edits before they are "done."

My favorite part of the mini-course is always the last few hours on Friday when we set a stool and a lamp in the front of a dark room and invite writers to read their final stories to each other. In those moments, the world becomes a lot less lonely.

We hope you will experience that same transformative support through reading this book, and that you will consider writing your own story. We are so honored to have you with us.

A Note from David Zwaschka

If this is a foreword, it's only to express gratitude to my colleague and friend Marjie Bowker for allowing me to participate in the amazing work she has begun, and to Scriber Lake High School's students for opening their lives and hearts—what a gift it's been to work with fifteen young writers so dedicated to their craft.

You may be struck by the harrowing nature of the following stories, told with such frank honesty. I have been struck by the kids themselves. They're *so* smart and funny, mature, compassionate, attentive to national and world events. (Ask them their thoughts on this year's presidential race if you have an hour and salty language doesn't faze you.) They *certainly* have strong opinions about the writing process and are more than happy to argue with you for an hour over the placement of a comma. But they have also experienced profoundly intense or painful events that add a weight to the daily effort of navigating adolescence.

If you're a teacher, you recognize our students in your classrooms. They might appear completely in control, masters of their fate and future. Or they might not say much (or too much), attend inconsistently, seem distant. With 150 students, who can know? I know what Marjie would say: Ask, then encourage a response in the narrative form. She's done so much terrific work in this field already, including shepherding four previous books through the publication process. If you're interested in learning more, check out her teacher's guide called *They Absolutely Want to Write*. It changed the way I think about teaching the narrative genre.

Writing a book—and the writing process generally—isn't all sunshine and rainbows. Painful life events, some unresolved at the time of publication, can conjure strong emotions. But working through their stories invited students to confront particular events *and* more transcendent questions such as *How do I explain to* myself *what my story is, exactly? How can telling it help my life move forward?* and *Can my story help others in similar situations?*

Like Marjie, I most enjoy the last-day's reading, when students share their work aloud and receive well-earned recognition in return. For that afternoon they are in the presence of others who have suffered their own slings and arrows, who are finding a way to new understanding, and who know what it means to stand up and say so.

What an honor to have been there.

PLUS I LOVE YOU

DANIKA HENSON

"*We're sorry Danika. You're too good for this.*"

My parents' words have been circling in my head all day. Earlier, they were apologizing to me while the three of us smoked in the Durango. I know what they're sorry for: they're sorry for making us homeless. They're sorry for all the drug addicts I've been around at the motel. They're sorry for the way their drinking has caused so many problems. They're sorry for arguing all the time.

They want me to have a better life.

For the longest time I didn't want a better life—I didn't want a life at all. I didn't want to do anything. But now I do.

Hours after that conversation I'm sitting in my best friend Sarah's room writing a song about my life. A G-Eazy song plays in the background while she helps me with each line. We've been writing together for the past eight years.

Today, I have to get this one out.

"*Mother and Father been tellin' me I'm too good for this shit, I'm gonna luck out,*" I write.

When I write songs I like to use my life in my lyrics. I always knew those days at the hotel would count for something.

·❀·

"*We was raised in that fork in the road, no food on our plate just the meals that we stole...*"

Sarah, Ariel, and I were sitting in my mom's Durango—our sometimes makeshift home—in the parking lot of Andy's Motel with Mac Miller's words blasting. I was rapping as loudly as I could, even though I felt like I couldn't breathe.

"I spit that prayer hand emoji..."

I could relate to that line: praying for better days. As I looked at Room 44 straight in front of me, my heart pulled down from my chest to my stomach. I knew my parents were behind that dark green door with the white numbers, and I knew they were passed out, drunk.

"And this pain, mixed up with this rain, this rain, this rain..."

Sarah's bright red hair was bouncing and Ariel motioned to the music with one hand. Sarah and Ariel were like my sisters; we wanted to be rappers, and we thought Ariel's sweet, simple voice would make a great chorus. We called each other's moms "Mom" because we were always together. They called my dad "Asshole" because he was always angry.

"Let's go in and get something to eat," Ariel said when the song ended.

I realized I was hungry—we'd been in the car for two hours.

We entered Room 44 to find my mom and dad passed out on one of the two queen beds. The room stunk like cigarettes, beer, and hard liquor. My dad's Vikings hat and shoes were still on and my mom's hair was still up in her clip. This was an all-too-common sight for us, so we decided to grab food from the black mini-fridge, turn on MTV and lie on the other bed.

My dad woke up with his familiar pissed off-look. He lit a cigarette and grabbed a beer out of the fridge. When my mom woke up she was angry, too.

"Can you stop moving? I'm trying to sleep!" she said.

All of a sudden my dad yelled, "Where are the fucking keys at,

Danika?" When my dad was pissed, he left his mouth open and his bottom teeth exposed. I didn't take him seriously, though, because he never really looked at me.

"Dude, fucking chill," Sarah said back at him jokingly.

"Yeah, Asshole," Ariel added with the same tone.

If he hadn't been drinking he would have thought it was funny, but he got up and started throwing clothes around looking for the keys.

"What the fuck?!" my mom screamed.

"They lost the keys!" my dad yelled.

Sarah and I got up off the bed and started looking with him.

My dad got in front of us and yelled straight in our faces. "Don't ever touch the keys again. You understand me?"

My mom jumped between us, her long curly hair falling out of the clip, and yelled, "Shut up, Mark. They're probably in here somewhere. I don't know why you're freaking out on the girls!"

My dad went to push her out of the way, but Sarah stepped in front of her and quickly pushed him back. He had a crazy look of surprise on his face. His eyes got really big and his body tensed like he was going to hit Sarah.

My adrenaline was pumping and before I knew what I doing I gave him a right hook to his mouth. I felt his two front teeth cut my knuckles open. As he fell back onto the bed he looked at me with shock. I was shocked, too—especially when I saw the blood coming from his mouth.

⚜

I might as well call Sarah's house my own. I'm staring at the posters of Mac Miller and Marilyn Monroe we stole from the mall, which hang on the blue and green wall in her room. There used to be a picture of Thomas the Train there, but we covered it up with poster boards full of lyrics from our favorite artists: Eminem, Macklemore, Mac Miller. Their songs mirror my life and have encouraged me to keep going. They all lived through so much pain and suffering, but managed to come out so strong.

Because of them, I know everybody has a story, and it's time to write mine.

Sarah and I are talking about the night when my dad almost died, and what the next lines to my song should be.

"You know 'Neon Cathedral'?" Sarah asks.

"Yeah," I answer. " *'Shaking til I'd get a taste, my faith is having seizures.'* I like that line."

And then I write my own:

"*Dad's shaking violent, I hear the sound of sirens, This ain't how I want you dyin'.*"

I think about how sick he got—a few years before we lost our house.

✦

I woke up to my mom screaming in horror. "Doug!"

Probably just arguing with Dad again, I thought to myself. But the screams didn't stop, they were a cry for help to my uncle.

"Doug! Call 911!" she screamed again.

I jumped out of bed, pushed my door open and ran to the living room where my mom huddled over my dad. He was leaning over a bucket full of blood. His side had been hurting for months and he covered up the pain by drinking all day, but this was the first time he had thrown up blood. My face got hot and I couldn't find any air to breathe. I watched as he struggled his way to the recliner chair to wait until the ambulance arrived.

The firefighters and paramedics rushed in moments later.

My dad looked up at them and said, "I feel better now. I think I'll wait to go to the hospital." For how sick he was, I was surprised at how completely fine he looked.

"I don't know, Mr. Henson. I think you need to go tonight," the first responder said. But it was useless; talking to him was always like talking to a brick wall.

"I don't want to miss Christmas," he said defensively. Being together for the holidays was a priority for my family. We cut down our own tree and decorated it with the same ornaments we'd been using since we moved from Iowa. For all nine years of my life, I got to open one present on Christmas Eve. I knew my dad didn't want to miss that.

The first responder turned to me with hope. "Is this your dad?"

"Yes," I said quietly.

"You need to tell him he needs to go to the hospital."

"You need to go to the hospital, Dad," I said firmly.

Because of his soft spot for his little girl, he finally caved. "Okay, Dani."

I watched as they put him on a stretcher, then into the ambulance. My mom and I followed behind in the car, and I started to relax. I felt like everything was going to be okay.

After hours of sitting in the waiting room while my dad had tests done, we were finally able to visit him.

His room was huge and empty, even with him lying on the bed in the middle of it. I hated everything about hospitals. The food, gross. The chairs, hard. The temperature, cold. The reek of staleness. I kept my eyes focused on the TV, watching an old baseball game nobody cared about with the volume completely off. I barely noticed the doctor coming in until I heard him clear his throat. I looked over to where he stood at the foot of the bed.

In a stern voice he asked my mom, "Mrs. Henson, what do you want us to do if he stops breathing?"

My muscles tightened and my eyes widened as they darted to my mom to see what she would say next.

"Keep him alive until our son can fly out," she answered in a quiet, shaky voice.

⁕

I grab my phone and put on Mac Miller's *Watching Movies with the Sound Off*.

"*My days get darker, so the haze gets sparked up…*"

I see Sarah's phone light up. The phone reads *Asshole* in big black letters.

"Hey, hold on, I'm gonna put you on speaker," says Sarah when she answers it.

"Hi, Dad!" I say.

"What's up, brats?" he says jokingly.

"Just chillin'. How about you?" I answer.

"Watching TV with the boys. Not much. I just thought I'd give you guys a holler."

I miss him a lot; he's been in Iowa for almost two years now. I miss taking the bus with him and making fun of all the people we see, and sitting in the car listening to Eminem waiting for Mom to get off work.

"Plus I love you guys," he says when we're saying goodbye.

"Love you too, Asshole," Sarah and I say in unison.

I wish I was there with him, my brother and my nephews. I want to be a family again. I think about the last time I saw him.

⁕

"Look at that clown over there," my dad said, sitting inside of Epply Airfield in Omaha, Nebraska.

I faked a smile and a laugh because we were always making fun of people, but it was hard for me to breathe. It was hot and humid, but mostly I was sad to be leaving my family. I'd been staying with my dad and my brother for the last month of my summer vacation in Atlantic, Iowa, where I was born. My dad and I were trying to make small talk to distract ourselves. I was leaving, and we didn't know when we would see each other again.

When people looked at my dad, they saw a big, scary guy who looked like he was ready to beat someone's ass. But I just saw my dad. He stood tall, wearing his black Vikings hat with a Nirvana t-shirt, a pair of Levi's and a fresh pair of Nikes. He really did look mean most of the time, but right then he looked sad. I'd only seen him cry once, and that was when he was talking about leaving my mom and me to go to Iowa. He decided to go because he was tired of being homeless, and my brother had offered him a nicer life to stop him from drinking so much.

Another flight was called on the loudspeaker, and I let out a sigh of relief when I realized it wasn't mine. We watched as a young woman reunited with her family. As they hugged I remembered how happy I was when I got to Iowa and hugged my dad for the first time in eight months.

My dad continued trying to make small talk, but I said nothing back. I didn't want to leave. I wanted him to come back with me so we could be a family again.

My flight was finally called and his blue eyes sunk in like he was about to cry. My nose started to burn as I held the tears back the best I could. I went to hug him one last time before I boarded the plane back to Seattle. He lifted me off my feet and squeezed me tight.

"Plus I love you, Dani. Stay out of trouble and don't get caught."

He'd said "plus I love you" for as long as I could remember: before I went to school, before I went places with Sarah, and even for no reason at all.

I took one last whiff of his Old Spice and headed toward the security line, tears already falling. I took a breath and a loud sob came out. I couldn't control it anymore. I felt everyone staring, but it didn't matter to me. I turned around one last time to say goodbye and as we made eye contact I wondered how many months it would be before I saw him again.

⁕

I hop off Sarah's bed, light an incense stick and stand beside her, looking out her window.

"What direction are we taking the song?" Sarah asks.

"Gotta talk about drowning in my sorrow," I answer.

"What about *'I'm drownin' deep six feet under and I'm barely movin'?'*"

"That's perfect."

"Read the whole thing back to me," she says.

"I don't know what to do anymore I'm so stressed out
this hoe goin' crazy outside
Mom's telling me not to flip out
Reachin' up under my bed into my bag to pull my knife out
Mother and father been tellin' me I'm too good for this shit
I'm gonna luck out
Police and paramedics rushing to her
Cause she's strung out
I'm hearing Ari calling my name
Or it's Sarah

I can't tell now
I'm struggling hard just to get a buck out
Come walk a day in this Love Pink
These headaches don't go away until I fall asleep
I've smoked weed, I've popped pills
ain't nothin' workin'
I thought a couple bucks would just stop the hurtin'
I'm questioning my life like ten times a day
my homie's dying
she keeps running away
I can't chill, I can't sleep
So I just
Lay awake
I'm drowning deep 6ft under and I'm barely movin'
They say if God brought you to it he can bring you through it
I heard drinking won't bring you to heaven
Don't know why I wanna do it
Dad's shaking violent, I hear the sounds of sirens
This ain't how I want you dyin'
I see the boys all crying at your funeral
Life's brutal but beautiful—"

"That's awesome," Sarah says. "God Speed" by Mac Miller comes on and we start singing along.

"Opened up my eyes, I'm finally awake, good morning…"

A Note from Danika

I don't want to make it seem like my parents are awful people, because they aren't. They're the best parents anyone could ask for—they encouraged me to write this story. Since this happened I moved in with my cousin, my dad came back from Iowa, and my parents and I plan to get our own place soon. I decided to write my story because I hated my life for a long time and I finally got tired of hating everything; I made a choice to be happy. I went from skipping school every day and failing all of my classes to getting straight A's. My goal is to graduate early and then study abroad.

"For what's money without happiness? Or hard times without the people you love? Though I'm not sure what's about to happen next, I asked for strength from the Lord up above, cause I've been strong so far." – J Cole

THEY

SHALYN ENSZ

"Do you even know why you're here?" the specialist asks again. His voice sounds worn and impatient, which doesn't do anything to help the slight nervousness I feel in this stale room. No windows, one light hanging above us and the obnoxiously shiny table make the room unsettling. The way his voice seems to echo off the white walls causes my anxiety levels to rise.

I feel Gloria's hand on my shoulder, warm and comforting as always. *"Don't tell him,"* she says. Her voice is reassuring and even though she doesn't talk much, her words have a way of putting my mind at ease.

"Shalyn? Are you still with us?" the specialist asks, tapping his pen against the wooden clipboard covered in chicken scratch.

Another voice, this one less comforting, speaks to me. *"You can't trust the people here,"* Lre warns. Lre is always trying to make my day more miserable, so this is just another opportunity for him to confuse me.

"Shalyn...? Shalyn?"

My eyes fly open and my attention snaps back to the bald man in the blue nurse's uniform. He's practically on the other side of the room because the table between us is about ten feet long. Is this for safety? Does he think I'll hurt him? I've never hurt anyone before.

Gloria is still standing behind me and I want to hold her hand, but given the situation, I doubt it would be a good idea. She pushes her glasses up and brushes back her dark, short hair as she smiles at me. *It's going to be okay,* her smile seems to say.

"I'm here," I say in a quiet voice. The specialist nods before scribbling something on his clipboard. He sighs for the hundredth time since this began, looking exhausted. It's only our second hour in here; I don't see why he's already like this.

"Why does he have a clipboard when there is a table to write on right there?" Lre nags.

"Quiet! Let her think, you moron," Gloria scoffs. *"I don't trust him either, but you're not helping."* She's always there to defend me when Lre is annoying. Even though I can't see him now, his presence in my mind is annoying.

The specialist sighs again. "Do you know why they called me in?" he asks slowly, as if I didn't understand the first several times.

I'm sure the "they" he's referring to is the psych ward staff. As to why, they are all worried about my imaginary friends, the voices, the ones that have been speaking to me for the past few years. They kept my status as "outpatient" when my mother brought me in only a week before, so obviously I have no idea why they've called a specialist. Just like every other kid here, I am dealing with depression and its symptoms, but the nurses haven't deemed it severe enough to keep me overnight.

"No," I tell him.

"You're a special case. Not everyone experiences the same things you do. It's *special.*" He mumbles on about how "special" I am and that there is nothing to be afraid of.

I already know this, though. Gloria has told me several times that she won't hurt me, neither will Toby or Zave. For about nine years now I have been "special." I am special because they talk to me, and no one else. Ever. Of course, they aren't the only ones who have talked to me—it's not always fun and laughter, like it always is with my "friends."

"Now, Shalyn, I'd like you to start from the very beginning. When is the first time you had this *special* encounter?"

It's embarrassing, being so open about this for the first time. I've never opened up to anyone about this before, not even my parents. I focus on the clipboard, the chair, the white walls, anything besides the specialist. I've never felt exposed like this before, but I know I have to tell him. I take a deep breath before going into detail about how it all started, back when I was five years old.

✦

I sat in my aunt's hammock on her patio. The one on the left. Always the one on the left because my older brother Isaac always got the one on the right. I didn't want that one though; left was better because it was closer to the ivy I loved to play with.

"*You look bored,*" I heard from the yard.

My head turned in the direction of the voice, but there was no one there. I ignored it.

"*Why won't you talk to me?*" This time when I looked over, my eyes locked with...a person? Was this a person?

"Vizzy?" The name came out of my mouth naturally. I didn't even have to think.

I had never seen her before in my life. How could I suddenly know her? By the time Isaac came out to sit in his hammock, Vizzy had already taken his spot. I was ready for him to have a fit or ask her to move, but he did nothing. He just sat down. Right on top of Vizzy.

"Isaac, ask her to move next time! Vizzy, are you okay?" I asked, jumping out of my hammock and running over to her in a panic.

Isaac looked over at me, his seven year-old face full of confusion.

"Who? There's no one here but us. Everyone else is inside."

"My new friend, Vizzy. She's special because only I can talk to her," I told him.

He still looked confused, but eventually accepted it. By the time I was nine I had Vizzy, Crystal, and Morgan with me. Over the course of the next few months, we would play baseball with them in our big yard. I started seeing more of these people, each with their own personality. Sometimes I would play with them at recess instead of playing with my classmates. The thought of playing with the same classmates every day didn't excite me as much as playing with these girls. Isaac would talk about his friends, too, but admitted he couldn't see or hear them like I did—that they were just people he made up. Our parents called them our "imaginary friends." Isaac's didn't last long before he gave up on them. But mine weren't really imaginary.

⁂

"So they haven't always been harmful, then?" the bald man asks.

His questions are repetitive, just like this entire week. After stopping at McDonald's every morning for a breakfast sandwich and orange juice, turning in any objects that could harm people, and about an hour of waiting for the rest of the outpatients to show up, I would be taken to a separate room where I would do inkblot tests and the like. I always ended up in the same stale room with the same questions.

"We're not harmful..." Gloria reassures me, though it seems she's trying to reassure herself more than me.

"No. It wasn't until a couple years later when they became harmful." I try to remember details, but my memory has never been very good to begin with.

Over the next hour I tell him about the time I was about eleven, when I stopped seeing Vizzy and the others with her. They would no longer visit me at night when I couldn't sleep, hold my hand as I walked to the kitchen in the dark for a glass of water, tell me jokes in class when

I was bored, or assure me that they would protect me from the shadows that always crept towards me from corners in the ceiling, the ones they called "K." They didn't come back for about a year, but when they did they were different. Their names were Toby, Zave, Max, Holly, and Gloria. Like the first few imaginary friends, I didn't have to ask them questions about who they were. They were different, though, because they all had their own being: speech patterns, clothing styles, haircuts, voices, sexual orientations. They were like real people. Toby had black hair and didn't talk much. He really loved Max, who was a very short girl with freckles, bright green eyes, and a voice that could bring you to tears. Zave was Holly's younger brother and they were both blonde and tall. They stayed with me all day and night, never leaving my sight or my dreams. I didn't mind, though; they were there for me when my mom was in alcohol rehab and my dad had just gotten remarried to my current step-mom.

After hearing about my parents, the specialist asks, "Did your family situation affect your 'special' friends?"

I'm not sure whether it was my family situation or my insanity that affected them. I tell him this and he nods, scribbling down everything I say. I swear he writes just as fast as I speak.

"It wasn't until 2012 that they really started to change my life," I tell him.

He looks up at me from his notes. "Can you elaborate?"

"They started to tell me what to do. Sometimes it would include hurting people or worse."

⚜

"We'll take you away."

"You'll what?" I asked the figure sitting on the edge of my bed.

I didn't recognize this being as a friend. I didn't even recognize them as a human, no gender or specific voice. They were turned away with their head down, reading my copy of *Maximum Ride: School's Out Forever.*

"I said we'll take you away, Kat." They still didn't turn around.

I was confused. Who were they talking to? Who was Kat? Was she a new friend? I didn't have to say what I was thinking out loud for this strange being to hear.

"You," they said, just barely above a whisper. *"You're Kat."*

"I'm not, though. I'm Shalyn." I leaned further against the back of my chair, a nervous feeling creeping into my gut. I knew I shouldn't keep talking, that I should break this conversation off and ask Toby for help. But I was too scared.

"You don't have to be Shalyn anymore. You hate it here, just as much as we would, right?"

"'We?'" I repeated.

I was still very confused, and they could see that. I didn't know why but something about this being made me want to believe every word that rolled off their tongue. What they were offering was exactly what I had been wishing for for so long. I had been longing to find some way to change my situation, whether that was failed attempts at running away or locking myself in my room for days, only leaving once or twice a day for food. Escape meant being away from my step-family, my school, and my mom's absence in rehab. What reason did I have not to accept?

So I became Kat. Shalyn was only someone's body I was trapped in until my friends would come and get me and bring me away from wherever I was.

"Have you accepted who you are?" the figure asked.

Answering with a "yes" was probably the worst thing I could have done. From then on my mind went numb for about a month and all I could think of were two things: I wanted my mom back out of rehab, and I wanted Gloria and the rest of them to take me away.

"If you want them to come, you have to give something up."

"Give what up?"

"You know where the scissors are, right? The green ones you keep in your second drawer for the posters you make."

"What do you want me to do with them? They don't do much but cut paper." I tried to talk quietly because everyone else in the house was sleeping.

"Go get a knife instead, then. One of those big ones from the kitchen, Kat. It's what Kat would do. You want out, don't you?"

I nodded my head, but my hesitation was still visible.

"I know what you think of your step-mom and her sons. I've heard what they say about you. I've seen the messages he sent you."

They were playing on my weakness; I had felt hatred for my step-mom ever since she moved to Washington to marry my dad.

"I don't know," I said, a bit more cautiously.

"You were there. On the stairs. Don't tell me you've forgotten already."

The voice was sounding more and more vicious, deep, and demented as it spoke to me. Unlike the rest of them, this one had no form, just a dark image that appeared in my mind as they spoke.

Suddenly it wasn't that voice I heard in my head, but my step-mom, Maryanne's. *"Marc, she has to go."*

And then my dad's voice answering her. *"I know, I'll go talk to her."*

My dad and step-mom wanted me gone. They wanted me far away from them. I knew it and so did this thing talking to me.

My mind went numb and I couldn't think straight. I remember a knife, silent tears and the panic every time I made a noise while I was trying to remain unnoticed. I blacked out soon, only to wake up the next morning with aching arms and a tear-soaked pillow. It was a Friday, and I didn't leave my room until the next Sunday when my brothers and I went back to our mom's apartment with our aunt. I liked her small apartment, although I didn't talk much for fear of revealing what I had just experienced. If I did, my aunt may have called a priest; her only explanation for the voices in my head was demons or possession. Growing up in a religious environment, what other explanation was there for this to happen to a child?

We were allowed to visit our mom in rehab for part of the day, but other than that we didn't see her for another couple months.

It was another year before my parents noticed anything, and my mom—out of rehab for most of that time—decided to take me to Fairfax after a suggestion from Rachel, my therapist.

✦

There's a knock on the heavy wooden door and the bald man's assistant comes in with boring-looking paperwork—apparently my results from the inkblot and other tests. Most of what he explains is confusing, like how to read the results and what all the big words mean. All I can focus on are the big letters and the graph that reads: PSY: 68% SCH 98% MDD 80%. There are others, but I don't pay attention to them.

"What does the s-c-h mean?" I ask, already knowing the other two mean *psychotic* and *major depressive disorder*.

He looks down at the papers for a moment, then back up at me with a solemn expression.

"Schizophrenia."

When the word leaves his mouth, I let out a breath I didn't know I had been holding for years. It's not demons, it's not a punishment, and it's not even unheard of. There's a word for it. Which means there's a way to deal with it.

Finally. I finally have my answer.

A Note from Shalyn

I would continue to believe I was Kat for the rest of my time at the private school I attended and about halfway into my first year at public school before finally snapping out of it with the help from my new "friends"—whom I won't name. What happened to the rest of the ones mentioned is part of a darker side to my hallucinations that I don't talk about, though fortunately that has not happened in over a year. I still have occasional flashbacks of what happened that night with the knife, but for the most part it is all behind me. I am extremely happy where I am right now; in fact, I've never been happier. After opening up about this to more people and writing it out, I was shocked to find that it isn't as off-putting as I thought it would be. I realized it's pretty common. Some people I told were interested in finding out more about what goes on in my head rather than shunning me like I was used to for so long. Another reason I wrote this story is to break the stereotype that people with schizophrenia are noticeably different or completely gone. I have accepted that they are hallucinations, but that doesn't make them any less real for me or anyone who goes through the same thing. By accepting that they are a part of me and may never go away, I have opened my eyes to a new view on life and I've learned that you don't have to get rid of what's part of you with medication or therapy if you can learn to tame it yourself. As for the future, I plan to graduate early and teach English as a second language overseas. Writing this story has helped me start working toward that goal.

"Writing is a socially acceptable form of schizophrenia."—E.L. Doctorow

PLANS

COLE MOORE

The dull natural lighting in the kitchen is not ideal for writing suicide letters. My body is scared—shaking and sweating—but my mind is clear and focused. This afternoon is my last. The sparkles from my pen mixed with tears smear across my left hand as I write line after line to my mom, dad, and dog, Wesley. *"Words cannot describe how much I love you guys. I'm simply not ready to grow up..."*

Unlike his usual lethargic self, Wesley is scratching frantically at my leg, almost begging me to stop my sad thoughts. He's trying with all his might to heave his tiny, nine-pound body onto my lap. But my mind is set.

I'd rather be dead than a loser.

This is for the best.

I give some thought to my parents, hoping they won't be too sad, but I realize it isn't about them, it's about me. Few people have ever loved someone as much as I love myself. I'm simply doing this to protect me.

I need to do this.

My favorite green polka-dotted glass is filled to the brim with water and a matching green bendy straw sits on the table surrounded by 33 Prozac, the strongest medication in my house. What was once prescribed to help me is now about to be the cause of my demise two years later. Pill number one sits between my fingers as I contemplate my decision. "Dance with my Father" by Luther Vandross plays repeatedly in my head, just like it did when it played at my grandpa's funeral when I was five. *Is God sending me a message? Is this my time to go?* Wesley always knows when something is wrong. He tickles my leg with his dull, overgrown claws.

I ignore him and focus on the pill.

I don't want a bad life.

With my lips on the straw I slowly swallow the first pill. I instantly pick up the second and from there my arm works like a well-oiled machine, grabbing the pills and catapulting them down my throat, counting as I go, relaxing more as the number gets higher. With each tiny capsule, I'm released from my fears of adult responsibilities. After pill number 33, I get up from the kitchen table and walk to the plush living room couch.

I take the biggest blanket off the arm and sprawl out. Before I can spread the blanket over me, Wesley is standing on me with his bony paws, ready for our usual after-school nap. He quickly burrows between me and the cushion and I lay comfortably with Wesley for the last moments of my life. I was taught suicide was an unforgivable sin at my Christian school, but I also know God loves me. He loves us all, he created us and he forgives us, even for our worst mistakes. I squeeze my eyes shut, praying to God that he'll forgive me and take me to his kingdom in my sleep.

My phone is off to avoid the call from my boss telling me I missed my shift at the shoe store. I'm completely relaxed, my fear of being a failure is disappearing as I stroke Wesley's shiny black coat, drifting off into the silence.

⚜

I wake from my slumber to see the popcorn ceiling that I know is not heaven. "Fuck!" A wave of relief crashes over me knowing I'll see my best friend again, my mom. But the wave quickly dissipates at the thought of school on Monday. And then I realize the pills just haven't kicked in yet.

I can't have my mom come home after a hard day's work to discover my lifeless body.

I have to get out of the house.

I kiss Wesley's forehead, search for my car keys and head toward the door. Wesley sits on the arm of the couch, wagging his tail as I happily wave to him like usual, trying to ease his small mind of any worries.

I attentively watch my beloved BMW's soft top fold down into the trunk for hibernation, a fascinating process I know I'll never witness again. There's nothing I love more than cars—they're my life. Especially my car, the best 16th birthday present my dad could've given me. I work my engine like a slave, paying close attention to the beautiful sound as it propels me and my machine down the asphalt at full force. My last drive is bliss. I am on my way to God only knows where.

Muscle memory takes me on a very familiar route, to my high school. A thought hits my mind. *They're the ones who drove me to this point, so they should have to find my body, too.*

Earlier that day I sat in Spanish class feeling like a confused moron. I was failing all my classes and was about to fail another test. In that moment I realized I'd rather be dead than an uneducated adult with no future and no money. I knew exactly what I needed to do. My plans for a great life—a good college education, a great family, nice cars, and a nice house—were quickly crumbling before my eyes. I knew I would have to demolish them myself all at once rather than watch them slowly implode.

I park under the shade of a tree in the school parking lot. The smell of my car's abused tires and brakes invades my nose as I watch afternoon track practice. My eyes dart around, squinting at all of the kids running around the big black oval in the hot sun.

I hope they don't think I'm a creep for watching them.

But my paranoid thought is soon replaced by an even worse one: I realize my plan is most likely a failure. Fearing my overdose won't kill me but instead just cause complications, like paralysis, I decide I'd rather be fully functional and sad than disabled, miserable, dependent and sad. I quickly sort through my options: *I don't want to die. I can't tell my mom. Calling 911 is not a good choice—I can't deal with the medics alone.*

With a decision made, I drive to my Aunt Patty and Uncle Paul's house, just a few blocks away. I know I can always confide in my aunt; she helped raise me while my mom worked. At a young age I was always by my Aunt Patty's side, singing in my car seat, playing in the yard, or just laying my head on her lap. Since I transferred high schools, I've been seeing her a lot more again.

I swing open the squeaky front door and dash up the stairs to the kitchen, like usual. Aunt Patty is happy and surprised to see me, and my uncle is at the counter eating enchiladas.

"Hey!" he greets me.

They think I've come to celebrate Cinco de Mayo with them, but my aunt's demeanor changes when I bluntly say, "I need to go to the hospital."

"Why? What's wrong?" she whispers, terrified. "Is this a suicide thing?"

She knows I've been to the hospital before for having extreme suicidal thoughts, but that I've never acted on them. Embarrassed, I nod and slowly mumble a confession of my actions.

"How many did you take?" her voice rises in panic.

"Thirty three."

"Oh my God!"

I stand dead still, inhaling the scent of the freshly-made enchiladas, watching my world like it's a movie. They move like Olympians putting on their shoes, grabbing bags, keys, and calling my mom. I can hear her heartbroken tone over the unusually loud phone—a sound that would normally bring me to tears—but now has no effect.

"What hospital do you want us to take him to?" Aunt Patty asks, followed by, "Okay, Children's."

No thoughts go through my head as I sit in the back seat on our journey. I am emotionless. For the first time in my sixteen years of life, the freeway of thoughts in my head is completely empty. My mind is as grey as the headrest I'm staring at.

The irony is that my family is trying to save me but I'm already long gone. The happy kid I once was has now been replaced with a motionless mannequin.

I can no longer recognize who I am.

A Note from Cole

After six days in the hospital I came to the realization that I was putting unnecessary pressure on myself to succeed. I returned to school for one day in the spring, and on that day my Spanish teacher suggested I transfer to Scriber and write my story. I am now thriving at Scriber, where I will graduate on time next year. Writing this story has brought back a lot of bad memories, but I am very proud of the person I've become over the last eleven months. I am bettering myself every day. I hope everyone knows they have at least one advocate to help them through life. I'm finally awake after realizing how many people are here to support and cheer me on; all I had to do was ask. I plan to go to college and pursue a career as an automotive journalist. I dream of one day being on TV, hosting my own show about cars.

ANY LAST WORDS?

ALICIA VERZOLA

"Kylee told me stuff about you and your mom," Austin, my boyfriend, says.

My heart drops to the bottom of my stomach and I feel like I'm going to throw up. It's pitch black out and the car windows are foggy from us talking for hours.

"What did she tell you?" I ask. But I don't really want to know. I wasn't *that* close with Kylee, so I have no idea what she knew about my mom. But the fact is it's been four years now and anything to do with my mom still affects me deeply.

"She told me you used to beat up your mom all the time. Is that true?"

Austin continues to talk, but I can't focus on the conversation anymore. All I can think about is what else people think about my mom and me. When we got into physical fights, most of the time I responded belligerently back at her and screamed so much I didn't even know what I was saying anymore.

Did it even look like I was defending myself? Does everyone just think I fought her for telling me to clean my room? Everyone must think I'm evil.

I want to get out of the car and run away. All other people remember is when she was not herself, because she wasn't herself when she was drinking. The only memories I want to keep of her are the ones when she was happy, like the moment on Christmas Eve four years ago.

✦

My mom struggled down the stairs behind my cousin, gripping the side rail. I watched, embarrassed, her tights making her slip on the tile as she made her way to the couch. She had taken her heels off five minutes after we arrived to celebrate Christmas Eve at my aunt's house.

"Hi, Mama," I said. I hadn't seen her since we arrived because it was too stressful being around her. I wondered if I should go upstairs to get away. She drank more when she got nervous, and she was never more nervous than when she was in front of our family. She wanted to impress them, but she always ended up getting drunk too fast and digging herself into a deeper hole.

Earlier, I had pretended not to hear my aunts talking about her in the kitchen. She had been upstairs visiting with my great grandma who was nearly deaf but who smiled and nodded anyway. My mom always liked it when someone would listen and pretend like she wasn't slurring her words. Everyone shot me *sorry* looks. It had been the same every year for fourteen years. Embarrassing.

"Hi, baby," she said to me, falling on the couch next to my cousin. She reeked of perfume; the mouthwash on her breath was a sad attempt to cover the alcohol.

Then she noticed my cousin's new hat.

"That is just so cute!" she said. I could tell she was struggling to keep her eyes open. She had been nodding off all day. "Where did it come from?"

Everyone was smiling and laughing, eating and talking. A light Christmas carol played in the background and candles were lit all around the house. A Yule Log flickered on the TV. Everyone was dressed up and my little cousins were trying not to act uncomfortable in their dresses and sweaters. We probably looked like a family in a Hallmark commercial.

But my mom kept pulling down her dress that was way too tight and continued to focus on my cousin's hat. "I've been looking for one like that!"

Finally he took it off and handed it to her. "Merry Christmas," he said, annoyed, but knowing it would make her a lot happier than it would make him.

"I love it! It's so cute! Thank you so much!" She reacted like a child opening a present.

I hadn't seen her that happy for a long while. It was pretty embarrassing, but I was happy for her. She loved it.

⚜

"Okay, let's talk about something else," Austin says. "I want to be happy with you."

"Me too," I say, but I can't stop the thoughts. I can't focus on anything else.

What would've happened if I had just left during one of the fights? What If I had just let her hit me? Would she have been the one to get in trouble or arrested instead of me? What if I hadn't tried to keep her alcohol away from her? Would that have stopped the fights?

When I was younger, I didn't know. But eventually, after all the times I accidentally mistook her drink in the fridge for mine, I knew. At an early age I learned to smell my drinks first.

"Are you cold?" Austin asks, noticing my shivering.

"No. It's hot in here."

My anxiety is giving me an adrenaline rush. I stick my hands under my legs to keep them from shaking and try to focus on the cold leather against my knuckles. Anything to get my mind off that phone call.

❖

My boyfriend's phone read *Ali's house*. I blew my breath out as I walked into the back bedroom and stood in front of the mirror, looking to myself for advice. I didn't want to answer, but I knew I'd have to sooner or later. I assumed it was my mom trying to guilt trip me into coming home again. I knew I wouldn't be able to stay mad at her.

I took another breath. "Hello?" I said, letting the annoyance come through. But a male voice answered. It was my dad.

"Ali?" He sounded relieved that I answered. *Why was he there on a Thursday?* He usually only came over on the weekends. *Why was he at my house?*

"What?" I said with more focus.

"I need you to come home. Now." I assumed he just wanted me there because he wanted to see me. I didn't really care, though. I figured I would go home some other time. But I could tell by the tone of his voice there was more.

"Why now?"

"You just need to come home."

We went back and forth like this for a while.

"Why?!" I finally pleaded. "Why, why, *why*?!"

He took a deep breath and said, "Ali, your mom passed away today."

"That's not funny!" I yelled.

Silence.

How can he say that to me? Why is he trying to hurt me? How dare he? The sentence felt like poison.

"I'm serious, Ali," he said. Silence. I still didn't believe him. Like when someone says something mean to you, I just tried to not let it bother me, to ignore it.

"Okay, I'll come home."

I hung up the phone, my head spinning. My hands shook but I wasn't cold. *What made him say that? What was he trying to save me from?* My parents always sheltered me, more than they needed to in an unhealthy way, some would say. Maybe he was trying to make what really happened sound not as bad. He always did that, bad news then good news to make the bad news not so bad.

I walked out of the back bedroom and made it about ten feet when it hit me. I stopped and the hallway turned into a tunnel, it just kept going. I looked next to me at the bedroom, hit the doorframe as hard as I could, fell into it and then onto the floor. I was mad. Mad at her. Mad at him for saying that. Mad for what I said to her yesterday. Mad I don't understand.

I let the tears fall. *There's no way he's serious.* I felt like I was hovering over my body watching all of it happen, like a ghost. This wasn't real. It was a dream. I'd had this nightmare before and it always felt so real. But this time it didn't feel real at all.

✸

I feel like we've been in the car for days.

Austin keeps trying to find a way to talk to me. "Why would Kylee say something like that?" he asks.

The thoughts in my head exhaust me.

She was my best friend and I don't think I told her that enough.

She always told me to never go to bed angry, never hang up the phone without saying "I love you," never leave without saying "goodbye."

"You never know, what if I died tomorrow? What if that was the last thing you said to me?"

✤

We yelled over one another. I would've said anything to get her off the phone.

"Why won't you come home?" she asked, breathing heavily.

"I like it here and people aren't drunk all the time!" I screamed.

Her anger rose. "I'm tired of your excuses! You live here. You need to come home now!"

"I'll come home tomorrow, maybe. I don't know!"

She hiccupped before saying, "You don't get to tell me whether you are coming home or not!"

"I don't want to live there. I don't like it there!"

"You need to come home." I could hear the alcohol on her breath. "You don't have a choice!"

"I hate you! I'm never coming home!"

I hung up the phone. Whenever she was drunk, I felt like she didn't care about me. Why should I care about her?

✤

I hate you! I'm never coming home! I hate you! I'm never coming home!

The words play over and over. They won't stop.

"I need to go inside," I say to Austin.

I get out of the car and head to the door.

I told her I was never coming home again and I never did.

Home doesn't feel like home without her. Going to sleep isn't the same, either. Sleeping in the same bed almost every night was the best part of the day. We would put on our pajamas, crawl into her bed and lie next to each other, forgetting all of the drinking and the fighting. Nothing ever felt more like home than her bed.

I go into my room, fall into my bed and think the same thought I go to sleep with every night.

I wish my last words to her would have been "I love you."

A Note from Ali

Writing my story has been very hard. Struggling to put all the pieces together in draft after draft forced me to re-live it by going back and remembering events I tried to forget. I chose to go through this process because I wanted to experience the healing and support that previous Scriber writers talked about. It worked; writing this helped me deal with guilt and acceptance more than any counselor has in the past four years. My mother's death came after a year of conflict. In eighth grade, my best friend moved away; soon after that I dropped out of school and moved in with my boyfriend. I didn't expect to graduate because I never went to school. When my mom died, everything fell apart. My grandmother took me in and helped me get back on my feet, and then my dad and I moved in together and started making a home of our own. Thanks to the help of my friends and family at Scriber, I am currently on track to graduate this year; I don't think I would have been successful at any other school. Next year I plan to follow in my mother's footsteps and go to cosmetology school. Every day's a new day, and one by one I'm working to make my mother proud of me. I love her with all of my heart and, although I may not have told her that, I still move forward every day for her and because of her. I thank her for all that she gave me.

SHARDS OF GLASS

JOSEY DANIEL

The ice cold water feels like shards of glass on my skin, causing my jaw to clench.

I swear they do that on purpose.

I'm weak and helpless. The withdrawals make my skin feel soft and fragile, like an overripe plum. When they checked me in the officer gave me slippers three sizes too big and pants I trip over. I step out of the shower, throw on my oddly huge clothes, and walk out.

"Where do I go?" I ask the guard. I feel like a robot; all my movements are pre-programmed. I'm walking, but it feels like someone else is walking for me. She takes me to a room the size of a cubicle containing only a toilet and a mattress. My legs become heavy, lead-like. I feel small and tired.

The guard hands me a sack lunch. "I'll come get you when I'm ready to transfer you downstairs," she says in a tone of disgust.

How long is that going to take?

I sit down on the bed and pull out a sandwich—the bread looks discolored, the meat slimy. The apple should've been eaten a week ago, and I'm scared to drink the cup of juice. When I take a bite, the sandwich tastes like dirt and mold. I immediately throw up.

My body shakes, but I can barely lift the blankets to cover my body. I'm cold but I'm also sweating. Anxiety washes over me as I go through the events from earlier today.

Why did I have to punch her?

✳

"Apologize to me!" my dad's girlfriend, Ksenia, demanded as she lunged forward to grab me.

"I didn't do anything wrong!" I yelled. I tried to say this calmly, but it didn't come out that way.

Ksenia pushed me out of my room toward the bathroom. She was trying to stop me from leaving because she knew I would just go use.

"Stop! Don't touch me, you bitch!" I shouted, the smell of fresh detergent on her clothes making me gag. I hated feeling trapped, and I could feel the addiction tugging at my chest, pulling me toward my next fix.

Why won't she let me go?

My fight-or-flight instinct kicked in: I raised my fist and punched her in the nose. All I could hear was my own heart beating, and everything in my sight turned red.

She towered over me, flailing her arms—the size of twigs—and her hair moved around like a match in the wind. Her skin was so pale it blinded me as the sun shone through the window and reflected off her as her open hand hit me, but I couldn't feel the pain. I heard her screaming, but I couldn't make out any words.

"Get out, get out!" came through clearly, though, as Ksenia threw my clothes down the stairs outside my room. As I followed her down to the front door, I picked up clothing on every step. "Don't come back," she yelled. "I don't want you here!"

I heard the panic in her voice and saw the terror and anger in her eyes. It made me happy that she was scared of me. Even though I was still furious, I picked up the last of my clothes and shoved them in my backpack. I closed the front door and felt my blood rise.

What a bitch. She's not even my mom. She can't treat me like that. I hate her.

As I walked quickly to the McDonald's around the corner, the sound of bumper-to-bumper traffic on Lake City Way calmed me down. No one ever bugged me there.

When I got there I lit a cigarette and paced back and forth, listening to the sound of my rubber shoes scraping against the cement.

Where can I stay tonight? I don't want to sleep at the park again.

I had slept there a few nights before because my parents had changed the locks.

After smoking almost the whole cigarette, I started to feel the cold December air creep up my spine. I finished and stepped inside. I sat down on the green, plushy chair and texted my meth dealer, who had smoked so much heroin with me the night before that I couldn't even get up. I had been sure I was about to overdose.

I finished sending the text, then set my phone down and bit my nails nervously. Every time I put a nail in my mouth, I smelled tobacco smoke on my fingers.

I heard the door opening behind me. I turned around and panic washed over me: a young, inexperienced-looking cop was walking through the door. My hands started to sweat and I felt light-headed. I looked around thinking *where I can run?* But it was too late.

He approached me and said, "Miss, is your name Josey Daniel?"

The words hit me hard, along with the smell of the coffee on his breath. I had no way out. I felt like I was about to cry, but I wasn't going to let him see that. "Yes, that's me," I answered, almost choking on my words. *What's going to happen? Am I being taken to juvie?*

"You're under arrest," he said. "You have the right to remain silent."

My mind went blank as I felt the cold metal of the handcuffs on my skin, secured too tightly around my wrists. I became numb.

When am I going to get my next fix?

I was a 15 year-old girl addicted to meth, heroin and GHB—a brain surgery/date rape drug. I treated my family like dirt because I *wanted* to be a drug addict. I had been one for a couple of years, ever since meeting a boy named Tanner. I was in seventh grade, visiting my mom in Granite Falls, when Tanner gave me my first hits of heroin and meth. I had said "yes" when he asked because I was afraid of what he would do if I didn't. I was abused by him in more ways than one, so I thought doing these drugs would make it all go away.

I did GHB the next year. My so-called best friend put some in my vodka at my birthday party when I lived in South Seattle. I had gotten sick and was in the bathroom the entire time.

In ninth grade, I *really* started doing it. I was at a trap house with my friend, and we borrowed a friend's car and drove to Renton. At the time I didn't know where we were going, but when we got there, he told me he was getting some GHB. He put it on a cigarette, let it dry, and then we smoked it. It made me feel kind of drunk, but still in control of my body. At that moment I knew I loved it. I wanted more.

"Do you have any weapons?" the cop asked. I realized I had left my knife at my house, but I had a dime of weed in my breast pocket. If he found that, I knew it would be a possession charge. Tears started to build up again so I swallowed, attempting to get the metallic taste out of my mouth. I tried to look as normal as possible while he searched me.

I can't let him find it.

Luckily, he just patted me down, put me in the car, and went through my backpack.

Thank god he didn't find the weed.

But I knew he'd find a drug pouch in my backpack with a tooter, bubble and tin foil. He found the tooter and called it a "glorified meth pipe." I smirked to myself. *I don't know how you would smoke meth off of plastic without melting the plastic.*

He put my stuff in the trunk and got in the driver's seat. "I'm keeping this," he announced, gesturing to my drug pouch. Then he drove me around the corner to my dad's house.

His partner was already there talking to my dad and Ksenia, so he got out to join them. I watched through the car window.

Great, now I don't even have a chance to tell my story. No one will believe me anyway.

I felt the anger and resentment take over. I couldn't sit still and started to overheat. The arresting officer came back and took me by the arm out of the car to talk to my parents.

"Miss, you realize what you did was domestic violence, right?" the officer asked.

I turned around, got on my tippy toes and yelled in his face, *"I was defending myself!"*

Both cops threw me to the ground. One cop's knee was on my upper back, almost to my neck, and the other's knee dug into my lower back. I was too angry and full of adrenaline to feel the pain of my face pressed against the pavement or the weight of two full-grown officers pushing me into the rough cement. But I did feel the pressure.

My parents chose to keep me at home and not have me incarcerated. They wanted to give me another chance.

I waited a few hours, until everything had settled down and I was sitting in my room. I put my shoes on and tried to run for it, but my dad grabbed me as I tried to get past him through the living room. He called for my brother, who grabbed me by my legs, and the two of them dragged me back upstairs to my room as I kicked, scratched and screamed. When he shut the door, I threw a stool at it, stood on my bed and ripped my full-length mirror off the wall. Shards of glass flew everywhere. I had to leave.

I didn't want to feel the withdrawals.

I didn't want to feel the mental weakness of my addiction.

My dad heard the ruckus, walked back in and saw the damage. He pinned me down, so I tried to bite him. "Stop, Josey, just stop!" he pleaded with tears in his eyes, shaking me because I wouldn't listen.

"Get off me!" I screamed, lifting my head to get in his face. I only wanted to be set free.

While he held me down, my brother walked in and took my knives away. It was like watching movers bringing boxes in and out of a house. Being claustrophobic, I felt my anxiety hit hard; my breathing became uneasy and I could feel my stomach in my throat. I felt like I would die if he didn't get off of me.

"Get off! I can't breathe!" I yelled. I wriggled out of his grip, crawled to my window and flung it open with too much force. I heard a loud smack.

"Call the police," my dad said to Ksenia. I could hear the sadness in his voice as he tried to get me to stop hyperventilating. "I'm sorry. Josey, calm down. I didn't know I was hurting you."

I was sobbing, curled up in a ball, thinking *Life's hopeless.*

A different squad came. The female officer put me in cuffs and helped me get my shoes on.

"You're being arrested for domestic violence and malicious mischief," she said as she led me to the squad car. I saw my brother run down the driveway. I thought he was coming down to say goodbye, but he was only acknowledging that I was in custody. I clenched my fists, feeling betrayed, as he headed back to the house.

The ride to Alder Detention Center in downtown Seattle felt like it took four hours. I was furious with my family. *How could they do this to me?*

As we pulled into the fenced-in, gray facility with flood lights and cops everywhere, I felt the pain of abandonment.

My life sucks. Nobody cares.

A Note from Josey

I spent Christmas in rehab without my family, which was devastating. I woke up from that nightmare and changed who I was—now people no longer feel like they're walking on eggshells around me. I'm over a year clean, and I'm a completely different person. I've learned that the people who look like they're trying to hurt you could be the ones trying to help you, so it's important to take a step back and assess the situation. When I wrote the first draft of this story—one year after it happened— I cried because I still wasn't over what I did to my family. Writing it has helped me work past it, though, and I hope someone will read my story and try to change before things get too bad. When my dad read it, he was happy to finally hear my side, so it also feels like this is my chance to tell it how I remember. After a lifetime of problems with him, we are now hanging out regularly. Ksenia and I have found common ground, too; we no longer bump heads. I'm working really hard on respecting my family and myself. When I graduate in 2019, I'm going to become a writer because I want others to read my stories and learn from them.

THIRTEEN

SARAH JEAN

I swing my legs over my bedroom window sill, my strappy heels clicking against the pieces of wood I stacked under the window four hours earlier. I glance over at the fake people we made in my bed out of discarded clothes from trying on outfits all afternoon and then look up at my friend Claire, holding my pointer finger to my lips. She gets the point and flashes her mouth full of braces at me.

My phone buzzes. It's a text from Alex, the 17-year-old I've been with for almost three months. It says, *Hurry, I'm outside.*

My stomach turns from excitement. I'm with my best friend, my partner in crime, and we're excited to be hanging out with older guys.

Two windows down my grandma's lights are still on. She never notices I'm gone—or maybe she doesn't care. I've been sneaking in and out for almost three months now, which has become the new norm for a Friday. And after stumbling in drunk many times and forgetting to take my heels off, I'm almost positive she knows. Yet she pretends not to. She probably doesn't want to believe her thirteen year-old granddaughter is already sneaking out.

Claire takes off her heels, jumps down quickly, and we walk quietly around to the side of the house. I'm wearing a black pencil skirt and heels, she's wearing a tan and white pencil skirt with nude heels, and we have matching short jean jackets. We walk on the narrow path near the house until we get to the driveway. When I see his truck, a different type of adrenaline hits me. I clench my hands into fists so Claire can't see them shake, push the feeling aside and reason with myself. *He's never hit me in front of a friend.* I repeat this in my head as we scurry down the driveway, our heels clicking against the pavement. *Tonight will be fun,* I tell myself. But I can't get what happened a month ago out of my mind.

⁕

I walked with blistered feet down a silent road somewhere in Everett, drunk and tired, feeling only ache and burn.

It had snowed two days earlier and all I had on was a crop top, pencil skirt and heels. My outfit choice seemed reasonable for sitting in a warm car, but I had left my purse in Alex's car because the only thing I cared about at the moment was getting away from him.

I really wished I had my cigarettes. At least I had my phone, because I kept it in the waistline of my tight skirt. I had called Claire at least ten times, but it kept going straight to voicemail. I was on the verge of a panic attack. My breath was heavy, my face was red from the cold, and my hands were shaking from stress.

I collected myself and brainstormed options: I couldn't call a taxi without my wallet. It was 2:00 am so I wouldn't be able to get ahold of Claire anytime soon. I wouldn't be able to catch a bus until at least 6:00 am—if I found a bus stop, that is. The last thing I wanted to do was call my grandma and let her know her little girl was tainted, have her pick me up dressed like I was, smell all the alcohol on my skin, and see the fresh bruise coloring my collarbone.

I felt weak with my bruise exposed; I needed to get home and get my tattoo concealer on it. Alex had bought it for me after he hit me the first time. He had taken me shopping as a way to say "I'm sorry," and told me it would never happen again. He spent hundreds of dollars on me. When we got to the makeup store he showed me the tattoo concealer and whispered, "Look, babe, this will cover it. I don't want anyone to think

I beat you up."

At the time I was in a good mood. He had bought me a bunch of clothes and I didn't think hard on it. All I said was, "Okay, perfect," and went back to trying on lipstick colors.

I thought about calling Alex—he probably would have calmed down. I could get my purse back and smoke a cigarette. He'd been blowing up my phone with texts that said *I'm sorry*, even though most of them included the word "but" right after.

I opened one of his texts. It said, *I'm so sorry. You know I didn't mean to hurt you, but you know I have anger problems. You know that, baby.* I realized my only option: I picked up the phone and called him.

Before I dialed I thought to myself, *Just don't let him apologize.* I'd said that to myself a lot lately.

His pickup rolled up next to me ten minutes later, the apologies starting even before I got in the car. By the time we arrived at my house, I was back to thinking he was the best boyfriend ever and we made plans to go out the next night. He was always great with his words. When I snuck back into my house I was praising him in my head. *Everyone has problems. He's really a good guy and he's cute. He could have any girl he wants and he's with me. I just need to be a better girlfriend and be understanding.*

✧

Once we step out from the grassy side of my house onto the driveway, we adjust ourselves and walk swiftly to the street where we see Alex's black Dodge truck halfway down the block. He's blasting Ty Dolla $ign. We run down to the car. I head to the front passenger seat first, but Alex's close friend Johnny is there, so I climb into the back seat and look forward at my boyfriend. He has on a blue shirt, True Religion pants and a pair of blue and white Jordans. His hair is spiked with gel—I could run my fingers through it and it would stay the same. *I'm so lucky.*

Alex looks back at me with brown, glossy eyes and a half smile. *I think he's already drunk.* He's wearing an over-the-top amount of the Victoria's Secret men's cologne I bought him, which is a sign he doesn't want me to smell how much he's had to drink. He bites his lip— which means he wants a kiss—so I lean forward and press my lips on his. As our lips touch, I get a strong whiff of alcohol. My palms get sweaty and my anxiety kicks in. *Almost every time he's hurt me he has been drunk.* But when I look in his eyes, he doesn't have *the* look.

He seems completely relaxed, so I allow myself to relax too. *This could be a good night.* Johnny turns down the volume. He's here so Claire doesn't feel like a third wheel, but she has never met him before tonight.

"Want to go to the beach?" he asks in a strong Spanish accent.

I look for Claire's reaction and her eyes tell me she's up for the adventure, so I nod my head in agreement. I had gone to the beach with Alex just a day or two ago, and we had had a nice time. We weren't drinking.

Johnny looks back at Claire, checks her out and hands her a half gallon of Grey Goose vodka—a quarter of the way gone. I catch myself staring at Alex's strong arms, wishing he would hold me in them and assure me over and over that he'll never leave me or hurt me again.

Claire lifts the heavy bottle and chokes down a large gulp, then passes it to me. As the bottle reaches my hand, Alex makes a sharp U-turn and quickly speeds up to 90 mph on a back road. He's blowing stop signs, not caring about his surroundings. I feel a rush; I am not worried about my life or hitting something or how drunk he is, I am just enjoying it. I feel grown up and free. I want to feel like this forever.

The bottle spills and trickles onto my skirt, but I don't pay attention.

I put it to my lips, filling my mouth and swallowing over and over again, my worries fading with each gulp. After a while I pass it to Claire, who does the same. We pass it back and forth all the way to the beach.

When we pull in, Alex parks crooked, opens the door and stumbles out. Claire and Johnny do the same. I'm the only one who unclicks a seatbelt. The ground feels like water when I step out and I fall. Claire comes to my rescue, laughing hysterically.

"Someone's drunk!" she says as she helps me stand up. I hold myself on the truck to gain balance, then run over to Alex and start kissing him, holding his arms to maintain balance. Claire and Johnny go down to the water, and I just smile when I see them walking away side by side.

"Want to get in the car?" Alex asks, watching me wobble. I laugh, and without a word I walk around the car and open the passenger door. He looks at me dead serious, giving me chills.

"What were you doing all day? You weren't answering my texts." He's angry, but he isn't at 100% yet. I think for a minute and respond. I tell him the sequence of events.

"Babe, my phone died at two, I couldn't charge it until I got home at six, then I left and met up with Claire and we were busy getting ready until you picked us up. And you were working all morning."

He doesn't say anything and I can tell by the dead look he gets when he's angry that he's not satisfied. *I should have tried harder to let him know what was going on.* He hands me the bottle and changes his mood too quickly. He smiles as he says, "Take some shots with me." This gives me relief. I chug the bottle and pass it back. We do this in silence for five minutes until he grabs my head, pulls me toward him and kisses me.

"Get in the back with me," he demands. I get the spins. The alcohol is taking over and my stomach feels like it's churning. I feel dizzy, like I've been spinning in a circle 1,000 times.

"I…don't want to. I don't feel too good. We're in public!"

His smile disappears and he gives me another cold, dead look. He throws his hands up and says, "All you ever do is make excuses. You're my girlfriend. You need to start fucking acting like it."

"I just don't want to mess around right now."

"Whatever. You never do." He opens the door, gets out, and slams it. My body jumps from the loudness. My heart beats a million times a minute and my mind races for answers and ways to make him feel better. *Am I being a bad girlfriend? Do I have to do it with him? Should I just do it with him?*

I get out and hold myself up on the car as I walk around to the other side. He's leaning against the car, puffing down a cigarette. I try to hug him. "I'm sorry, babe."

He throws down the cigarette and grasps my arm tightly. I see the look in his eyes and I feel overwhelmingly distressed, like I need to flee. But his grasp and my balance won't let me.

"I need someone to show me they want me. You always have excuses. You don't love me."

But I do love him. I think I love him.

"You know I love you. I just don't…"

His eyes and face are completely blank. The beautiful smell of the beach and seaweed is covered by alcohol and Alex's cologne.

"You're hurting my arm," I say. I try to pull away again, but I can't get out of his grip. He shoves me hard against the car and I hit my head. "Please stop! Alex please…"

Before I can finish his knuckles hit my jaw on the left side of my face. The sand, stars and water look like muted tones of grey, black and blue as I fall to the ground. For a second, my vision is blurry and my ears ring loudly. I catch my breath and taste stale, bitter alcohol on my tongue.

I feel vomit coming up from the back of my throat and my stomach contracts.

I lay on the ground, dizzy and emotionless, gravel in between my fingers. When I look up all I see are his size eleven Jordans walking away toward the water.

A Note from Sarah

While I was lying on the ground, the only thing I could think about was getting fixed up because I didn't want anyone to see me like that. Once Claire came back from the water and saw me, she went into protective best friend mode. She took me to the bathroom and helped me clean myself up, then she made them take us home. I was crying the whole way, while Claire cussed at Alex. When we got home she comforted me while I poured my heart out about everything. That night when I fell asleep she took my phone and blocked Alex from everything (Facebook, phone calls, texts, Twitter and Instagram). I had no clue she had done that for a few months, so I thought he just wasn't texting me or responding. When she told me I was mad at first, but quickly realized it was the best thing she could have done. I haven't seen Alex since that night. He knew not to come to my house because my grandma wouldn't approve of our age difference. "The look" I referred to in my story is something anyone who's been through domestic violence situations knows. People don't really talk about "the look"—not online or in movies or support groups; it's the look he gives you warning you to brace yourself, the look that stays with you forever, even when the guy's gone. It will make you flinch when you see a similar one, and it will come to you in your dreams. You can't escape it. When I first wrote this story in ninth grade, I felt a huge weight lifted off my shoulders. Writing it helped me wake up and take action for myself. I ended up telling my sister and then went to counseling to learn how to cope with it. Now I'm in eleventh grade and I'm publishing in hopes that it will help anyone going through something like this. I'm currently in a relationship with a great guy and we've been together for a year and a half. I plan to graduate in the spring of 2017, then go to school to become a medical assistant.

HAPPY BIRTHDAY, PEANUT

ARIANNA CARR

"**A**re you gonna talk to him?" my mom asks. She quickly glances at me and then returns her eyes to the road.

"I don't know," I answer as I stare out the window. That's what I always say when I don't want to talk, or when I'm around new people. I hear a familiar song on the radio but tune it out, listening instead to the cars whooshing past us as we drive down the freeway. We're on our way to Southcenter to see my dad, my real dad. I haven't seen him in eight years, but just recently he starting talking to my mom again. He's been sober for a while now.

A few weeks ago I received a card in the mail from him for my fifteenth birthday. I opened it and took the hundred dollar bill out, feeling empty. Was this somehow supposed to make up for him not being in my life for eight years? Like that could be made up to me with a hundred dollar bill. I looked at the card: *Happy Birthday, Peanut.* I missed him calling me "Peanut." I missed having him in my life.

Now he is about to be in it again.

As we get closer to the mall parking lot, I feel butterflies grow in my stomach. My heart pounds in anticipation as I watch the cars parking and leaving, thinking about seeing his face for the first time in eight years.

How is it going to be? I wonder. *Is he going to be how I remember him? Has he changed? Did he lose weight? Does he have tattoos? Is his voice still the same?*

I think back to when I was six at my grandparents' house, sitting in the living room with him watching *Spiderman*—a movie I knew my mom would never let me watch. Then walking back to the movie rental store, me in my yellow raincoat and rain boots, holding his hand with the movie in my arms. I think about how I never got to see my parents together because they divorced before I was born.

I don't remember when my mom told me about my dad being an alcoholic; I just always knew. That's why my parents weren't together, why I didn't see him anymore. The more recent years were the worst— he was doing drugs and drinking, gone, not living at my grandparents' house. We didn't know where he was or what he was doing.

I know my mom wanted me to think about my dad as a good man and not hate him for the things he'd done, so she didn't tell me the stories until I was older: how he would burn up her things when he got angry, how she had to call the police when he tried to kick in the back door, how he failed to pick me up for visits when he was supposed to. How he would start a new job, but then lose it because he was too drunk to go to work.

And I knew my mom resented that my older brother, Jon, had such a messed up childhood—being picked up from school by a drunk father, or walking in on him while he was watching porn. One of her friends had threatened to call CPS, saying she was being neglectful of my brother by keeping Dad around. My mom told me she used to take my brother for long walks at night just to get away from him.

I look over at her as we drive in silence. I notice her short brown hair, slowly turning grey. I notice the wrinkles on her face, probably caused by stress. She's the one person I can usually talk to about anything. She is the closest person to me. But right now I don't say a word.

We park the car and that's when I see him. I take in his appearance: he's still skinny and short, with tattoos on his dark arms.

He walks over and greets us. "Hey there," he says with a smile. He doesn't seem nervous at all. I notice that he has a chipped tooth.

I wonder what that's from. Could it have been from work? Or something bad, like drugs?

"Do you wanna go to Olive Garden?" Mom asks, breaking the tension. She knows that's one of my favorite places, and she loves the breadsticks.

I quickly agree.

When he gets in the car I have no idea what to talk about, so I continue to say nothing. *How do I talk to a man who is almost a complete stranger to me? How do I get back the time I lost with him?* I wish things were how they used to be when I was six, when the words would just flow out of my mouth. When I could talk to him like he was one of my best friends, and when he would make me smile a toothless grin. I remember him taking me to a Blue's Clues concert, buying me a light that lit up and spun around. I played with it long after the concert because I would smile at the memory of that day. I remember him walking me around Rite-Aid, letting me pick out a stuffed horse that was as big as I was and buying it for me. It still sits above my bed.

As we follow him into the restaurant, I notice that he still wears the same type of light-washed jeans he did when I was little. We sit down at a booth, me by my mom and him on the other side, and my legs begin to shake against the hard, cold seat. I don't say much during lunch; mostly, my mom and dad get caught up on things. I answer when he asks me questions, but all I give is short, one or two-word responses.

"So how are you doing?" he asks as he turns to face me. I look into his dark brown eyes.

"Good," I say with no emotion. I look down at the floor next to the booth and they continue their discussion.

I look over at my mom. I watch how she keeps smiling and laughing—the light little laugh she's always had. She looks happy, like she isn't stressing or worrying about anything. Usually, she's stressed all the time.

"Thank you," I say when it's over. I'm being polite because he paid for it.

Before we go back to the parking lot we stop to get gas. My dad gets out of the car to talk to my mom at the pump, then walks away from her and pulls out a bag of tobacco and a cigarette he's pre-rolled himself. He has always rolled his own cigarettes. I don't like it that he smokes, but I would rather him do that than something worse.

My mom comes back to put her debit card back in her wallet. "Tom has something he wants to give you," she tells me.

I get out and walk over to where he's standing. He hands me three hundred-dollar bills.

I look down at the money in my hand and feel the same emptiness.

"What do you say?" Mom demands, her lips forming into a hardened line.

"Thank you," I say quietly.

"It's for school clothes," he says with a smile.

Is this how it's always going to be? Is he going to just give me money?

"Oh, okay," I say, not knowing what else I should say or do. It feels wrong, like I'm taking money from a stranger.

When we drop him off at the parking lot, we say goodbye and I watch him get into an old, blue truck.

On the drive home, my mom turns to me. "How do you think it went?" she asks.

I know she wants me to say that it went well.

"Good," I tell her, not really wanting to talk because I have so much going on in my mind. *When am I going to see him again? Will we get close again? What's going to happen now?*

"Him giving you money is his way of telling you he cares, that he loves you. That's the only way he knows how to do it," she explains.

I pause a moment before speaking. "Oh," I say.

So this is how it's always gonna be.

A Note from Arianna

After meeting with my dad that day I've been talking to him more. We don't have a great relationship, but it is better; we text more and we have lunch every few months with my mom. I decided to write this story because I needed a way to move on to a new chapter in life. After writing it, I felt I could build back a relationship with my dad. It will never be how it was, but I am hoping that I can still have him in my life. Writing my story has helped me to be more open and talk more freely with people about what's going on, and I feel more awake to the realization that moving on is for the best. Most importantly, I am no longer holding onto negativity. I moved out of my mom's house and now live with my boyfriend and his sister's family. I am on track to graduate on time, and plan to go to college to become a neonatal nurse.

THE SOUND OF GOODBYE

DANIEL COHEN

Climbing through the open window of my second floor bedroom, I know this has to be done. The wind hits my face for the first time in a year and a half and it feels so good—until I look down. I realize my fear of heights all over again as the open space stretches in the moonlight, making it seem like a thousand foot drop.

I can't be in this house, in this room, anymore.

My confidence building, I dangle my legs over the ledge. I turn to hold onto the window sill, lowering myself further into the open air.

Living on the street can't be any worse than being locked in my room. I just need to be free.

Thoughts of the abuse I've endured for the past eleven years override my fears as I continue my descent.

※

Walking home from the third grade at North Star Elementary, I experienced the same feeling of dread I had every day: the deep insecurity of never knowing what was going to happen.

Am I going to get hit? Am I going to be beat with the belt? Will I get dinner? Will this be my day off?

I knew my neighbor down the street, John, was home and had probably gotten a new game for his Nintendo 64. His mom was always nice to me, too; she treated me like family whenever I was around. As I trudged along the sidewalk, I thought *Maybe I should stay there for an hour or so. What harm could come from that? Maybe she won't notice if I get home a little later than usual.*

An hour of playing games went by in seconds. It was time to go home—I knew I couldn't avoid it forever. As I walked up to the house, I saw my step-mom glaring at me from the second story window. With each step, my fear grew stronger.

Well, here I am.

I opened the door and there she was, waiting for me at the top of the stairs in her pink lace nightgown and Winnie the Pooh slippers. I was an hour late. "Do you know what you did today?" she hissed, as if I was supposed to know.

Feeling my saliva turn sour, I whispered back, "Um... no?" Many possibilities went through my head. *Is it because I'm late? Is it the Pop Tart wrapper I left in the trash? Did I walk too loudly through the house this morning? Maybe it was the cup of water I left on the counter?*

"I found the pills you were supposed to take this morning. You forgot to take them."

My ADHD medicine.

"I told you that you needed to take your pills every day. It needs to be a consistent fucking habit. Damn it, Daniel, you know what's going to happen, don't you?" She took one step down and motioned for me to come up the rest of the way.

"Yeah, I know. I need to be hit," I responded with a sigh as my hands started to shake in fear. *Please, not again. Last time this happened I couldn't sit for a week. Please, no.*

When I made it to the top of the stairs, she grabbed me by my collar and pulled me close enough to smell the stale odor of her breath. My body went limp—I knew not to fight back. Fighting would only make things worse.

"What did I tell you about sighing?" she yelled into my face as she threw me into the hallway. My head bounced against the wall, dazing my eyesight. I wanted to crawl away to escape, but my body wouldn't work. I couldn't move. The walls started closing in as her 300 pound structure walked towards me. I struggled to see her—or even move my head—as I felt a sharp pain in my side.

"It pisses me the fuck off!" she yelled as she kicked me again, placing her hand against the wall to brace herself from falling.

Lying on the ground in pain, I thought about how I actually brought this on myself. I had picked her, after all. When I was three and my brother was seven, my dad had called us over to the computer and pointed to pictures on an online dating site. "Which one do you want as your new babysitter?" he asked. We both chose her picture; we were excited to have a new mother figure in our lives. He married her soon after. A few years later, the abuse started.

She kicked me one more time before deciding that I'd had enough. "That will teach you," she wheezed, out of breath.

Does this happen to everyone? Is this what people call home? At least she didn't use the belt today.

Knowing better than to say a smart remark out loud, I mumbled quietly, "Teach me about what?"

Recovering from the pain, I fell back into thought. *Why do I wait for her to stop and not fight back?*

Her heavy breathing distracted me from my thoughts until she yelled, "Go to your room! I'm done with you."

Well, no dinner tonight.

✦

I try to escape the sight of the drop by looking up. *I'm not ready for this.*

I don't even know where to go or what to do. I try to pull myself back up, but my hands are sweaty with fear and they slip, making me fall onto the concrete driveway below. Landing wrong, my feet go out from under me and I end up on my back—my big, heavy coat pockets full of clothes not providing the softer impact I had hoped for. I feel sharp pains in my ankle and head as I stare into the night sky.

I must have broken something.

Despite the pain, I get up and walk it off.

I limp past my dad's '78 Charger and onto the sidewalk that leads to the gate into the back yard. The house seems so dark and empty. It's the middle of the night and no one is awake except me walking this lonely path towards salvation. I walk deeper into the dark shadow the house casts, unlock the gate as quietly as possible, and shuffle toward the shed. My ankle throbs, but I ignore it.

If I can get my bike I might be able to make it somewhere before people realize I've left.

⚜

A few months into my ninth grade year my step-mom decided I needed to stay home and entertain her through her newest form of punishment. School was one of my only escapes, along with when my dad came home—the abuse happened less often then. But my dad was gone for months at a time for work, and when he was home, he wouldn't stand up to her. He was a Cohen, he told me, and Cohens didn't have spines. My brother had been kicked out months before, so I was officially alone.

Instead of going to school that day, I knelt on the porch with my arms straight out from my sides, making a straight line from fingertip to fingertip that strained every muscle.

I would have preferred a beating; however, the last time she hit me she left a huge black bruise on my face and almost got in trouble with CPS. So instead she left me outside in the harsh mid-winter winds of Washington. She made me sit on the bare, unpainted wood of the deck in nothing but my boxers just to prove an imaginary point that I could never seem to grasp. She glanced out every so often to make sure I was still on my knees. If I wasn't, she told me another hour would be added to my time. Every once in a while I risked a stretch, but I wondered if I might have to stay there overnight.

My only concern about her new game was whether I could hold my arms out for such a long time, but eventually they went numb due to the muscle pain and freezing cold. With snow clouds overhead, I stared into my reflection on the glass sliding door as her words rang through my head: "If I can't beat you, then 'She' can. Mother Nature does one hell of a job."

The wind picked up, seeming only to pierce my skin and chill my bones. Yet I remained untouched. I knew that the cold could only freeze, the heat could only blister, and the wood under me was hard, but that I had become harder. Not even time had a grasp on my sanity, for I was patient. Waiting. Watching her laugh at her show, watching her laugh at me, watching her watch me stare back at her, all the time thinking, *You can't get to me.*

※

My rusty bike—the one I've barely ever used—leans peacefully against the wall of the shed. I pull it out, push it through the fence and out onto the road. With each step the pain becomes more unbearable, spreading throughout the left side of my body. I'm barely able to swing my leg over the seat of the bike, but I push off and start pedaling down the road. The feeling of freedom is both foreign and exhilarating as I ride past the houses on my street. The air feels great—until the pain in my ankle forces me to admit:

I can't go any further.

I will never be free.

At the end of the street I start to cry—not due to the pain, but because I can't move on. I slowly come to a stop, realizing how foolish I was to try in the first place.

✦

My dad had forgotten to lock the window.

It was six days after my sixteenth birthday, and I sat in my empty room with only a mattress on the floor, a twenty-five gallon Clorox bucket in the corner for a toilet, and a surveillance camera by the door. I hadn't left my room in a year and a half. My step-mom had been granted permission to homeschool me, then installed locks on the outside doorframe and windows to make sure I couldn't get out. Most of the time I sat in the middle of the room talking to myself, looking at the white walls, knowing I had officially gone crazy. Occasionally I would lie on my back and count the bumps on the popcorn ceiling, wondering if I had been forgotten by everyone.

But my dad had opened the window to air out the room, and then closed it without going outside to lock it. The moment I realized this, I knew the only way out was through that window. I stood up and walked over to it, sliding it open as fast as I could, feeling the cold January air.

I can't take this anymore. I need to escape.

✦

I turn my bike around, giving up my dream of being free. I stumble to John's house because it's the only safe place I know. I lie down on their porch. It's cold and dark, and a droplet of rain hits my face. I lie there for another few hours staring into the night sky, letting the rain seep into my jacket and jeans.

I fall into the dark clouds that fill my mind. *What will my parents say when they find me? Maybe I should just kill myself. I won't be missed. I don't have friends. My family doesn't want me. Death would be better than going back, wouldn't it? I hear that heaven is great…but what if I go to hell?*

I'm nodding off deeper and deeper when I hear the front door open.

"Daniel?" a familiar, concerned voice says from behind me. John's mom places one hand on my shoulder and the other around my waist. With her help, I limp into the warmth of their living room.

A Note from Daniel

They say that demons come into our lives and that we need to deal with them ourselves. Otherwise, we carry our own burdens and bear them for all eternity. The demon in my life was my step-mom, but she is no longer my burden. I stayed with John's family for about a week because his mom took me in as one of her own. I contacted my brother—who had recently moved out—and asked to live with him; I knew I couldn't be at John's house forever, because they lived too close to my parents. Every day I stayed, I ran the risk of getting caught. Now I am living with my brother and we are both much happier. Because of this abuse I was basically two years behind in high school, but with hard work and dedication, I plan to graduate next year as a super senior—hopefully with all of my priorities straight. It was hard growing up so fast because I never really learned how to "adult"—it's been quite a learning experience. Looking back, I realize that the abuse my brother and I endured by our step-mom wasn't normal, and that's why I chose to write my story. I hope to show people that things can get better, even in the darkest of times. I plan to someday write a book about what happened in order to help leave the past behind and to show that there is a future ahead. Thankfully, I am finally awake.

COUGH AND COLD SWEATS

ANDREW EKSTEDT

I grab a twenty dollar bill out of my dad's wallet and pull out the creases. *Am I going to use this for food or drugs? Either one will satisfy my appetite.*

I scribble a quick note explaining that I've run away for the weekend, how sorry I am and not to worry. I place it on my hide-a-bed in the living room. My friend Cayman waits outside the door of my apartment while I steal Dad's money. We've been best friends since freshman year, so he knew me before my habit dictated the life I live now.

I put the wallet back in Dad's coat pocket.

I hear scratching at the door and Cayman's hushed and hurried voice through the crack. "Come on, let's go!" he says, nearly yelling.

"Dude, shut the fuck up. You're going to wake him up," I whisper.

I put the bill in my pocket and lurch to the door, slipping swiftly and easily through the crack. Sneaking out is natural for me nowadays. It's five in the morning on New Year's Day and I've been up all night. I can't believe we're actually doing this.

I remember the first days of this new, crumbling life of mine. The day I began to chase adrenaline two years ago, when I was fourteen.

❖

I felt the cold sweat pouring off my skin and down my neck. I was so anxious and excited, I felt like exploding. Laughter, happiness, and anxiety filled my stomach like razor-winged butterflies cutting their way up into my mind. I began throwing open kitchen cupboards looking for something—anything—that could make me high. I barely noticed crackers, chips, cereal and macaroni flying past my peripheral vision. I turned briefly to see food strewn across the linoleum flooring. Aside from my fixation, all was irrelevant.

I fucking found it—Triple C's, cold medicine.

My veins pumped adrenaline through my body, blanketing me in accomplishment and anticipation. My friend Adrian had told me that this could make you lose any sense of reality. I believed him, having seen him on it. I grabbed the pillbox and looked on the back. Exactly what I wanted.

Dextromethorphan, nothing else. No risk of overdosing. I pulled out the aluminum sheet and popped out the pills. Lying on my bed, I chewed the shitty-flavored tablets and swallowed them all, put on "Infected Mushroom" and waited for the high to kick in. The pills were crumbly; I was lying in powdered sugar and DXM.

A little over an hour later it kicked in completely. My teeth shook and my eyes vibrated. The only thing I cared about was how high I was and feeling the synthetic happiness. I walked to the bathroom and looked in the mirror. "Holy fuck, my eyes are the size of baseballs!" I said to myself in a cut, shaky voice. Life felt disjointed, the sequence of things mixed up and making little sense. I wanted to continue exploring it. I lay back in bed in a lull of euphoria and flashes of dreamlike thoughts.

I made my bed this way and now I have to dream in it.

❖

Aboard the bus with a shaking leg and an equally nervous friend, I turn to Cayman. "Do you think we're close to the Space Needle yet?"

This is one of the main reasons we ran away, to explore Seattle together. It feels like escaping prison. He takes a few seconds to respond, distracted by what's outside the window. "Yeah. We're in Fremont right now, so it shouldn't be too long."

I turn to look at the outside world. I think of how my dad will feel when he wakes up to find me gone. I've been making his life hell for a few years now; he's tired of witnessing my self-destruction. He probably isn't awake yet considering it's only 7:00 a.m. I can't keep the guilt from creeping in. *I can't keep running like this. I'm so tired of constantly avoiding everything. What the fuck am I even doing?*

"Hey, man, I'm going to listen to some music, is that cool?" I say to Cayman.

Again, he responds with a delay. "Oh, sure. No problem."

I put on my music and try to avoid my thoughts, but I continue to think about my father and what I've done to him and my family.

✦

I'm so fucking high my eyes are aching, so wide, so gone, you can't see my soul, it's lost. My skin is wax, I feel like I can melt, I feel like my body isn't here, I am not here, I can't feel anything. I am underneath the rainbow, talking to my friend. He wants to go on an adventure again; I tell him okay and smile. Mountainous regions surrounded by forests. We are laughing and I feel so alive and free.

I came back to reality in my bathroom. I had been sitting on the floor for an hour and a half with a Sprite Zero by my side and a toilet in front of me, the blinding yellow walls shaking in my vision. I lurched over the toilet again and vomited grape-flavored syrup, splattering the toilet bowl and every clean surface in the room. I could imagine my dad making a joke the next morning about projectile vomiting and how disgusting the room looked. He tried to avoid the thought of his son's absent personality by using humor. I understood. I left the bathroom and headed back to my hide-a-bed.

I heard him call me from the other room. I stood up, my legs trembling, muscles stiff. I walked from the living room to my father with a robotic movement similar to walking on stilts. He knew it too well. He bit his lip. "Hey, Andrew, you high?" he said with a cracking voice, trying not to cry.

I looked at him with iced-over, cracked, pupil-widened irises, "No, Dad, ha, I'm not," I answered in dissociated words, nothing behind them. I was running completely off of chemicals. I didn't exist. My stomach flipped, I needed to puke. I covered my mouth as I waddled like a robo-tripping penguin to the bathroom. I knew how stupid I must have looked. *I'm so fucking stupid.* I spewed more vomit over the floor and countertop. Why couldn't I hold it down? I was ruining my high.

I remembered my Sprite Zero by the toilet, unscrewed the cap and started drinking, tasting nothing but the carbonation. I fell out of myself and went to different worlds again. This is why I took the trips, the journeys. It was all about the escape from reality.

I'm going out hiking with my family again, we all are smiling, I have friends, real friends. I puked again and looked around at the crooked, surreal world. I turned my head and everything spun, similar to alcohol but with a much stronger intensity. I was on a merry-go-round looking out into the distance, unable to focus on anything. It wasn't real. I could be happy when nothing was real.

I heard my dad talking to my mom over the phone, her crying and him trying to calm her down, even though they hadn't been together for years. "What the hell are we going to do with him?"

I only heard murmurs of rage and frustration from the other side of the phone, my mom's tears and anger as she protested against my stupidity. "I know, I want him to stop, too, but I think we just need..."

I turned away from their conversation; if I listened I would have to think about what I was doing. I got up, legs shaking, lifting myself up off the puke-covered toilet. I waddled back to the living room and lay down on the bed. I put on my headphones and tried to go to different worlds.

I started separating from my body. I knew I was convulsing, but I didn't care.

It will be easier for them when I'm gone.

I saw myself from above and knew I shouldn't have taken 40 pills. It didn't matter. I came back to my body and saw my dad looking at me from the corner of his eye. He had been mentally preparing for me to die for the past two years.

I'm so happy that I don't have to think about being social with my parents. I'm so happy I don't have to think about my twelve year-old sister crying every day over losing me. I have never been this unhappy in my life and I want to kill myself. No I don't, I will just drift away and disassociate myself from the people who love me. Then they won't matter, then I won't matter.

⚜

"Hey, Andrew, we're here," Cayman brings me back with a shake.

"Oh, sweet. Wow. Holy shit."

As we exit the bus our faces are hit by sunlight and we both gasp, surprised by the blinding beauty of the city, the light reflecting off the glass windows. I've been here before, but never without the eyes of a nearby parent. I feel extremely happy, almost floating, as if I could fly. I realize that the shared isolation we both feel as we see the streets empty of people is a better high than I could ever achieve with any chemical.

The pavement is strewn with 2015 hats that were worn last night, piled nearly as high as our knees in some places. In the distance, the hats are being bulldozed into a much larger pile.

As we wade through them, I look around with new eyes. "So, what now?" I ask.

"Well, we could get something from that Walgreens over there," Cayman suggests.

"Yeah, I guess you're right."

Visualizing the aisles brings me back to my addiction. Ice pulses through my veins as my happiness is replaced by "the chase." My eyes go wild and my mind becomes hypersensitive; I only have one plan for that Walgreens. "Okay, so we're going to go in, I'm going to grab Delsym, and I'm going to put them down my pants, alright?"

"Uh, okay, sounds easy enough," he smiles back, but I can tell he doesn't really want to do it by the way he's scratching the back of his head and shifting his eyes. But he goes along with my plan to make me happy. Even though Cayman doesn't really enjoy getting high, he enjoys experiences. He'll end up drinking his bottle of Delsym later as well.

Recently, all of the time I've spent with friends has been focused on getting high rather than being with them. The last time I got wasted was a few days ago, the day I almost died.

✦

I chugged more Bombay. The room was spinning and I felt the need to puke even though I was laughing. About forty minutes ago I snorted half a Vicodin, but I couldn't really tell the difference between the three bottles of Delsym, the alcohol, or the pill. This was by far the drunkest and highest I had ever been. Garry and his friends were all wasted, stumbling over themselves in his house.

"Hey, man, can you get some Fireball?" Garry slurred.

"Yeah, uh, sure, dude." The words fell out of my mouth without any real structure. It was just the substance talking.

Soon I was walking towards QFC to steal some Fireball. I considered this a good idea, with my vision spinning and my head shaking. When I got to the aisle in QFC, everything went black.

I opened my eyes to be greeted by white walls and the discomfort of a vomit-crusted hospital gown. I still felt chemical energy pulsing through my skin and saw the world from a slanted angle. I had to pee so I tried standing up, only to find an IV in my arm preventing me. I ripped the tube out and stumbled out of my room to the front desk.

"Hey, um, where's the bathroom?" I asked the guy sitting there.

He looked at me with wide eyes. I looked down to see blood running down my arm, dripping on the floor from pulling out the IV. "It's, uh, right down that hallway and to the right, sir," he said shakily.

"Alright, thanks." I walked down the hallway to pee. Again, everything went blank.

I woke up to see a police officer entering the room, grimacing at the sight of me covered in my own puke. He stopped at the edge of the bed and glared at me. "Hey there, son. Did you know you tried to resist arrest?"

He looked at me sternly, in position for a quick gun or Taser draw. My eyes went wide. *Oh god, please don't let me get charged. My parents can't afford that after all of the hospital bills.*

"No. I don't remember anything. What happened?" I replied with a drawn-out breath.

"We found you on a street vomiting. When we pulled over and tried to arrest you, you tried fighting us off and we were forced to throw you to the ground."

That explains the head and shoulder pain.

The cop looked at me for eye contact, trying to intimidate me. I could tell he had endured a long night. "Well, we'll give you a while to sober up, then you can talk to your parents. You won't be charged this time."

He walked out and I let out the large amount of air I had been holding since the moment he entered the room.

❖

It's nearly ten in the morning—five hours since we left. I'm tired and weak from lack of sleep. I want to go home. I thought if I went out into the world on my own it would be an adventure filled with adrenaline and excitement. But now that my blood is done pumping, I just feel empty again. I always feel this way after I get the drugs—vacant until the next high or chase.

Cayman and I decide to give up and go home. He calls a taxi and we begin riding back. On the ride home, with two bottles of Delsym in Cayman's backpack, I realize I don't want this life. I don't want to go to jail, but most of all I don't want to die with a lack of personal accomplishment.

After I drink my bottle tonight I will never touch DXM again. I'm tired of being sick constantly.

We open the door to my apartment and hear that my dad is in the shower; he must have just gotten up. I turn around to face Cayman one last time before we part ways.

"Hey, I'll see you later, man," he says, smiling about our crazy experience.

"Yeah, we had fun. See ya, man," I reply as I slowly close the door, turning the knob to avoid noise from the latch.

The note is untouched on my pillow; he doesn't know yet. I'm relieved that I won't get in trouble, and that my parents don't have to go through the pain of me missing. I want them to see me start my new life.

I walk toward the bathroom feeling lighter. "Hey, Dad!"

A Note from Andrew

Two inpatients and outpatients later, I was finally ready to stay away from what would have eventually killed me, but the day of New Years was when I took the first initiative. I've been clean from cold medicine for a year now and feel much healthier than I ever have. I decided to write this story because I've seen so many people abuse cold medicine—nearly all of them unaware of the repercussions of their drug use. Writing this story was difficult because it forced me to look at the pain I've caused everyone, which I hadn't fully done since getting clean. My parents are finally proud of me and it feels good to achieve real accomplishments. I've recently gotten into hiking with a group called OSAT (One Step at a Time) and plan to climb Mt. Rainier within the next few years; now the way I fill my thirst for adrenaline is by climbing mountains instead of spiraling downhill. I'm finally happy with my life, which is awesome. Of course I have a lot of things that contaminate that happiness at times, but I can be happy with my imperfections, because imperfections are what make us who we are. Deciding to stop robo-tripping and choosing to associate with positive things and people rather than dissociate has made me wake up. I'm alive and ready to stay on my feet. After graduation I plan to go hiking as much as possible and want to use my own life experiences to help people better themselves as well.

POSITIVE

KARLA MARTINEZ

I feel my daughter's warm, small body on my chest. She is screaming, letting us all know she's here. The two women I love most in this world are laughing, smiling and crying next to me. My baby's father, Carlos, leans over my shoulder, rubs her fat cheeks and says, "Hola, Gorda."

As my mother adjusts Arianna's pink and blue striped beanie and takes our picture, I am filled with exhausted, relieved happiness; she has overcome the anger and disappointment of her fifteen year-old baby becoming a mother.

I think about the day the truth came out, when everything changed between us.

*

I heard the sound of an engine through my bedroom window.

Please don't let it be my mom. Please don't let it be my mom.

I sat up from my bed and saw her gray Durango pulling into our apartment's parking space. My heartbeat rose and I felt like throwing up. The car door slammed and I heard footsteps speeding up the stairs, which made my heart beat even faster. The front door opened and I knew her first stop would be my room. It felt like an eternity from the time I heard the door close to when I saw my doorknob turning, but that still wasn't enough time to think of what I was going to say. My mind was full of noise thinking about how my mother would react when I told her.

She walked over, stood next to my bed and asked, firmly, "Karla, estas embarazaba?"

The question hung in the air. I could tell by her strong pose that she was determined to get an answer.

How does she know I'm pregnant?

She always told me she would be there for me no matter what, and that I could trust her with personal things. I was sure this situation would be different, though, because she had high expectations for me and was very strict. I knew she had noticed a change in me over the past few months because she kept saying things like, "Your eyes don't shine like they used to."

Suddenly I wasn't her little girl anymore—she knew I was living an adult life. She even asked if I was pregnant a few times; when I answered, "No," she would say, "I'm going to be here for you, you know?" But she didn't ever expect this to happen. I was a respectful daughter, a good student, and president of my middle school. I had never been any trouble.

But I had known for a while, ever since the pregnancy test came out positive a month earlier. For four weeks I hadn't let myself believe that I was going to be a mother. Since then, I had been dreading this moment.

Answering "Si, Mami" used all the strength I had. I wanted to explain more to her and apologize, but I was speechless.

She let out a sigh and her body weakened. She stared at me in silence, which hurt more than a million words would have. Her eyes started to water and she looked away. I had just broken her heart.

My parents gave up everything for my sister and me. They left their country, their family and their lives to give us a future with many opportunities. My sister had been very successful; she was awarded a full-ride scholarship to Pacific Lutheran University to work toward her dream of earning a law degree. My parents expected even more success for my life because I had an earlier start—I was only one year old when we arrived in the states, and my sister was seven. My sister had done everything on her own, and I had the opportunity and privilege of someone to look up to.

But I had just ruined everything.

As she walked away, she turned around and said, "Eres una puta!" and then slammed the door behind her.

My mother had called me a bitch.

She had never spoken to me like that before. I felt I deserved it, though, and more. After all, her fifteen year-old daughter, her hope for the future, was pregnant, and she was experiencing a roller coaster of emotions. I tried holding back my tears, but once the first one broke free, the rest followed in a constant stream.

That night was miserable; never had I cried like I did during those long hours.

After that night, my mother stopped talking to me and my life became hell. Our relationship was gone. I didn't see her very often since she had two jobs and I was at school, but when I did see her, she seemed disgusted by my presence. She wouldn't even look at me.

Every time I attempted to have a conversation with her it ended in a full-blown argument. As each day passed I felt her love melting away. Her absence was too much for me—I was already five months pregnant, going through things that I didn't know how to handle on my own, and the woman I loved most refused to help. If my baby was causing so many problems before she was born, I couldn't envision what my life would be like when she arrived. I didn't want her to live in a home where people didn't love her, where she was seen as a disgrace.

The only thing I could think of to save my family was to not have my baby—or even better— to remove myself from this world. This thought was constantly on my mind; all I wanted was to live without worrying every second. The way my mother acted made me believe that she cared more about what others thought than how I was feeling.

✦

"Come on, Karla, she needs to feel that she is loved and that we want to meet her," my sister, Wendy, begged. It was her birthday, and my due date was fourteen days away. For months my mother had continued to avoid me.

Wendy had been asking to touch my tummy for months, but I hadn't let anyone do that besides Carlos.

Finally, after she persisted, I said, "Okay, fine. Go ahead, Wendy." As she placed her hand on my tummy, I could see the excitement in her huge smile.

"Arianna, soy tu tia! And I will be your favorite auntie in the whole world," she said as she moved her hand across my stomach with excitement in her eyes. From her touch I knew she was going to be an amazing and supportive aunt, just like she was as a sister.

What happened next took me by surprise. She called my mom in the room and said, "Mira mami tocale la panza a Karla."

I can't believe my sister is telling my mother to touch my tummy. She will never agree to touch me or my daughter, I thought to myself.

I pretended not to hear my sister; I didn't want it to be awkward when my mother said "no" or just ignored her. But she sat down on my bed. I sank down into a cloud where I couldn't see or hear anything because of how nervous I was, and felt the hard-working, soft, and loving hand of my mother touching my tummy. After all the weeks of not feeling the love of a mother, I was finally receiving it—even if it was only a touch. That one touch filled all of the holes that were missing in my life. Her touch replaced all of the weeks she wasn't there for me.

So many questions ran through my mind.

Why did she agree to touch me? What made her change her mind? How did she feel when she did? Was this just a one-time thing?

After my mother left, I was still shocked and didn't know what to expect from her next. But Wendy didn't seem surprised at all.

"I don't know where this is coming from," I said. Wendy began to explain that she had come to visit and found mom lying on her bed, talking to our aunt in Mexico. Their conversation had been about my pregnancy.

"What does mi Tia Mary have to do with her change?" I asked.

"Mi Tia explained to Mom how the absence of their mother while she was pregnant with Marely really affected her. That she would have given anything to have her mother by her side," Wendy explained. "She told mom to not take this opportunity for granted, and that even though you don't show it, a daughter will always need her mother."

My mother had always told me how amazing her mother was, that she was the most loving, soft-hearted and supportive woman. She didn't have the opportunity to say her last goodbyes to her before she passed away—it would have required her to risk everything to return because we were undocumented. She had stayed for us, and I knew how much pain was still stored inside of her.

I knew my mother was the same loving woman my grandmother was, but she just had to open up and realize we both did something wrong. And that we both needed each other.

⁂

As my mother removes Arianna's beanie and replaces it with a newborn hat that she purchased, she says, "Arianna looks just like you when you were born. Such pale skin with rosy pink and big cheeks."

Everyone wants to hold her, but of course my mother keeps winning. She continues taking photos and changing her into the many outfits she has bought. As I witness my family's excitement and demonstrations of love, I feel I can finally relax and be grateful. Seeing my mother hold my daughter feels surreal.

Arianna has arrived thirteen days early, and I know why. From the moment her grandmother touched her the night before, she knew she didn't have to hide and be afraid to come out anymore. She was ready to receive all of the love her grandmother had to give.

A Note from Karla

The bond between my mother and me is now unbreakable, and I wouldn't trade our relationship for anything. Now that I am a mother, I've learned to understand and appreciate my parents more than ever. Even though my mother wasn't supportive at the beginning of my first pregnancy, she was a tower of strength during my second pregnancy. My son's birth was very difficult—he was born seven weeks prematurely and had to stay in the NICU for a few weeks. My mother gave me the strength and motivation to stay strong for him; she was by my side through the most painful moments a mother can experience—seeing her baby suffer. My daughter is now almost three years old and my son is one and a half, and they couldn't have a more loving and supportive grandma. I am proud to say that even though I am an eighteen year-old mom, I will graduate on time this June because of my parents' support, my sister's words of motivation and Carlos' help with our kids. In the fall I plan to attend community college for two years and then transfer to the University of Washington to accomplish my lifelong goal of becoming a teacher. Teen moms, I want you to know that you are not alone in this hard journey. Don't give up because you are pregnant or have a baby. Your baby is not an obstacle, but a reason to continue reaching your goals. Don't let anyone tell you that you can't be a mother and a student, because we are warriors and warriors fight until the end.

PRIDE AND GUILT

TATAM WALKER

O n the way back to my seat, I look up and see Dylan's face. My gut wrenches as we make eye contact. Guilt. Goosebumps spread over my body. I didn't think he was going to show, even though I invited him.

A room full of my supporters are clapping, making me feel electrocuted—like a jolt of energy just shot through my body—because I have just received my key tag for having six consecutive months clean. I take a seat and look across the room at my parents. I know that if they were looking at me, we would exchange the familiar mixed emotions of pride and guilt; they are proud of me for having six months, but they are forever sorry for introducing me to this lifestyle.

I turn my gaze back to Dylan, who is now looking down at his lap, twirling his thumbs. He used to have an innocent, clean-cut appearance, but today his hair looks like it hasn't been washed in days and his deep brown eyes are surrounded by dark circles. His clothes are trashed—the stains are from god knows what and the holes look like he was bitten by a dog. My heart breaks.

Tears stream down my cheeks but I wipe them away before anyone can see them. The way he looks—it's my fault. Seeing him this way sparks the memory of the night I got the call.

❖

My phone rang next to me. I rolled over, pissed. *What the fuck? What now?*

I'd been awake on coke in a manic paranoia for over a week, and had finally fallen asleep. I desperately wanted to stay in that godly state, so it was easy to ignore the notifications that were woven into my dreams.

However, something was telling me I needed to answer the call, so I finally picked it up and said, "Hello?" in a groggy, defeated tone.

"Tatam?" a smoker's voice answered.

"Yes? This is she. How may I help you?" I asked. Even in exhausted anger, my customer service greeting kicked in.

"Okay. I just needed to make sure it was really you. There is someone here that needs to talk to you." I heard static as he passed the phone.

"Tay? Are you there?" Dylan's voice sounded small, worried.

"I'm here."

"I need you right now. I know you're probably busy, but I really need you." He stopped to catch his breath between statements. "My mom kicked me out and I have nowhere to go."

"What the fuck?" I asked, sitting straight up.

Dylan and his brother were the first people I met when I moved to Lynnwood from Port Angeles. They were the most understanding and welcoming kids, and I spent every day with them for two years. I certainly had never gotten a call like this from Dylan before. Any other night I would have gone and met him with no questions asked. However, this was the first night I had been home in over a week and any noise would alert my mom.

"Well, I can't do anything right now but I can come get you tomorrow. I have to do a pick up anyways so we can hang out for a while and wait around for Kyle," I said. Kyle was a dealer I had met through some friends. Dylan knew through the grapevine what my life had come to once again.

He paused before saying, "Okay. I'll meet you at the church next to my house at seven tomorrow morning. I love you, Tatam. Thank you." I knew what the pause was about; he hated that I was using again.

"Of course, Dylan. I'm not going to leave you out there. Just one night. I'll find you a place to stay tomorrow for a little while, alright?"

For the past seven months I had been living my life the same way I swore I never would again: picking up cocaine every few days and being involved with people I knew I shouldn't even give a second glance. I had thrown my life away again. Everything I had worked for in the last two and a half years of sobriety—getting my life together and staying away from drugs and gangs—was gone.

I didn't really care about what anyone thought about my drug use. I hid it from my mom because I didn't want to go to jail, but for some unexplainable reason, something always kept me tied to Dylan and his brother.

⚜

As the meeting comes to an end, we stand for the serenity prayer. I look around the circle but Dylan is gone.

"With an addict to my left and an addict to my right, I know I'm not alone," we say in unison. "God, Grant me the serenity to accept the things I cannot change…"

As we pull away, knots turn in my stomach as I pray for Dylan. "God, please watch over him. He needs you more than ever right now."

I'm heading home in the back of my parents' car when I get another call.

A deep male voice says, "Hello? Hello?"

"Yes?"

"Hi, my name Doug. I have Dylan here with me."

I sigh in relief. Dylan's drug of choice is heroin, so it's not uncommon for addicts to just drop.

"Is he okay?" I ask.

"Yes, yes he is fine. Well, as fine as he can be." The man seems to be mocking me. "You do know what he has been doing, don't you?" It's like he's rubbing the truth in my face. He's putting the blame on me. This man, whoever he is, knows I got Dylan into this.

"Yes, unfortunately I do. Does he need help? Do I need to come get him?"

"No, no, no," he says possessively. "He is staying with me tonight. He just wanted me to call you and let you know that he is safe and that he will call you in the morning."

"Okay... Can I speak to him now?" Something's not right. If Dylan wanted to talk to me, he would have just called. He wouldn't go through someone else.

"Uhm, no. He's, uh, sleeping. No wait. He's in the shower. I'll have him call you tomorrow."

"Wait!" I yell, but he has already hung up.

My mind goes back to the last time I saw Dylan before today.

⁂

I was curled up in the fetal position in my boyfriend Matthew's car, chin resting on my knees, body shaking from being dope sick. I just wanted to die.

I had barely remembered to tell Matthew we were stopping to get Dylan. He was right in front of the church where he said he would be. He jumped in the car with us, and we were halfway to the house when I got Kyle's call.

"Where you at?" he demanded.

"Almost there," I told him, my voice weak and irritated.

"Alright. I got all your stuff," he said.

"Okay." When Kyle started selling to me he told me that he would always end the call with the words, "I got all your stuff," and that if he didn't I shouldn't come because it might be a bust.

The house had a new coat of brown paint, so from the outside no one knew what happened on the inside. But there was still something uneasy about it. I heard Dylan mutter something under his breath, and I knew his reaction was judgment about my drug use. I gestured to him, asking if he wanted to come in, but he just stared at my blankly.

"Kyle is a family friend. Like a brother," I said. I knew that Dylan didn't believe a word coming out of my mouth. His head dropped and he gave me a "really?" look. He sighed and got out of the car, but Matthew stayed. He never came in with me and we never talked about what I was doing. He just drove me where I needed to go; it was a "don't ask, don't tell" relationship.

I knocked on Kyle's door three times, using the knock he taught me. The first was a subtle, almost "normal" knock, and the next two were harder and louder. I shook as I leaned up against the door, my jacket sleeves anxiously pulled over my fists. *I just want this to be over. I just want to get high.* Kyle opened the door just enough to see my left eye and then shut it again. He unlocked the deadbolts before finally letting us in.

"Close the door," I told Dylan after we entered. "Make sure to lock it." He did as I said, then took in the house—not a place you wanted to spend your free time. Every time I entered this house, I thought about how everyone said that it felt like people had died and were just standing there watching you. The interior looked like it hadn't been touched since the 20's, a contrast from the new paint on the outside. I pointed Dylan in the direction of the spare room where there were blankets, clothes, and a cupboard full of food.

For a moment, I had a sinking feeling that I shouldn't have brought him. But instead of worrying about that, I turned to focus on the issue at hand, which was making sure I gave the right amount of money to Kyle and that I received the right amount of cocaine back.

When the transaction was done, I yelled to Dylan, "Hey, I'm about to leave. If you want to come, you can. If not, I'll see you later."

He didn't answer.

I headed out the door to get high.

✦

The rush of guilt comes back. I know that if I hadn't introduced Dylan to that lifestyle, he would be sitting next to me in the back seat with my parents driving us home instead of with a stranger fighting his own addiction.

The recovering part of me starts composing a letter—the step where we make amends. I'm going over all of the things I want to say in my head: *"You were my best friend. I couldn't imagine my life without you. I know I made it hard for you to be around me. I really fucked up for both of us when I brought you to that house with me. I need to apologize to you."*

The recovering part of me hopes for our relationship to one day be restored, for him to forgive me, and to have my best friend back. However, the addict in me knows that one day at a time, the struggle will continue.

A Note from Tatam

It's been just over a year since that day. Two days after that everything came together and I started my road to recovery again. I think about Dylan all the time and have seen him briefly, but his addiction still has ahold of him. I chose to write about this because addiction and the guilt that goes along with it is something I struggle with on a daily basis. Writing this has helped me realize that Dylan's addiction is not my fault—that you can lead a horse to water, but you can't make him drink. In the end it is the other person's choice to pick up that pipe or needle. This is my senior year at Scriber and I can honestly say that I wouldn't be graduating this year if it weren't for Marjie and Scriber. I am currently going to school to be a special education teacher. I am finally awake; I am finally taking responsibility for my actions and my own problems.

DROWNING

KYANA REAP

"We love you very much, honey. We want you to know that," my father says.

We've been driving for three hours on our way from Shoreline, Washington, to Gladstone, Oregon, and I'm really starting to think my parents are up to something. They've given me everything I've asked for, including Starbucks coffee and a blueberry scone, and they're acting scared of me.

"Why do you guys keep saying that?" I ask, my throat tightening up.

"We just love you very much," my mother says. My hands shake and I fumble with my fingers.

It's just another therapy session, nothing to be anxious about. But why is it in Oregon?

My recurring nightmare—fresh from the morning—comes back to me as I stare out the window.

My family and I are standing on a beach. Everything seems totally fine at first but as I look around, nobody is there except us. None of us are able to move. I turn around and see the biggest tidal wave imaginable. Fear and panic wash over my body and everything moves in slow motion. I can't run. The wave inches closer and closer...

Each time I wake up before the wave hits, my heart tries to jump out of my chest from the fear of losing my family; I feel the same way now just thinking about it. I've been having this dream for a week, since the day I tried to take my own life.

⚜

I sat on the scraped-up, peeling wooden floor of my room and stared at the yellowish walls, hugging my knees to keep myself from losing control of all that I had left inside. I shook as I dug my sharp, uncut nails into my legs. My eyes burned and stung every time I opened them, so I kept them closed. I could hear nothing except my own thoughts—criticizing voices that kept screaming louder and louder.

You're fucking worthless!

You're a screwed-up piece of shit with no friends!

I tried to make them stop by drowning them out with my screams.

I glanced in the mirror across from me and saw a dark, reddish face with smeared makeup; I was fifteen years old and I didn't look anything like the person I once was. Pain and anger filled my whole body like lighter fluid on a fire. I stood, walked across the room, smashed my mirror against the wall and threw it outside my door. I heard the glass shatter.

I spotted the huge bottle of pain pills on my dresser, grabbed it and poured out a handful. I stared at them blankly, then forced them into my mouth and tried to swallow, but ended up choking and spitting some out. Dropping to my knees, I cried uncontrollably with the bitter, chalk-like taste in my mouth.

The voices continued to get louder. I gripped my head again and screamed to try to drown them out, but they filled my ears.

You have no reason to live, just kill yourself!

Each voice echoed in my head, causing me to try to rip my hair out.

I was done. I was done losing friends, then getting new ones who only made fun of me because I was some sort of circus entertainment for them. I never wanted to look at myself in the mirror again because I knew I'd see someone else. I felt I was becoming a sort of monster that destroyed everything in its path—like a corpse still walking the planet. Maybe I didn't feel like I was actually alive because of all the pills that numbed me and put me in this fucked-up state of mind.

I saw an empty jar across the room, stomped over to it, grabbed it and smashed it. A symbol of my life.

Killing myself was the only thing left.

I opened my door, shoved the mirror frame out of my way and walked into the living room, feeling the shards of glass dig deeper into my feet. My parents stared at me from where they sat on the couch, but when I glared at them they focused back on the T.V. They were tired of dealing with me. I dragged my bleeding feet across the wooden floor towards the kitchen.

Tears dripped out of my eyes with desperation. I wanted to let myself die without actually having to commit suicide, but I knew that wasn't going to happen. I opened the knife drawer, grabbed the biggest one and turned around to face my parents.

When I put the knife under my chin, my parents both jumped up in shock.

"I'm so fucking done," I said, choking on my words.

I took one last look, closed my eyes and slid the knife across my throat. My parents lunged at me and we struggled, but I finally let go and let them take the knife from me. All I accomplished was a slightly bloody scratch.

"What the hell are you doing, Kyana?" my dad yelled, terrified.

"I'm so sick and tired. Sick and tired of all this bullshit I've been put through!"

"You can't just kill yourself!" my mom cried.

I was familiar with the exasperated look on my parents' faces—they had put up with so much.

Why won't they just let me die?

"I can't live like this anymore. It's killing me."

I stood there shaking, wishing I could disappear.

⁂

As we continue our drive, I think about how long things have been bad; it seems like they've been bad forever. Ever since I was six, my parents have been saying things like "you talk way too much," and "stop talking."

Apparently, I would start conversations at all the wrong times. For years I had been prescribed different pills to treat ADHD, bipolar disorder, depression and crippling anxiety.

Even if the medication controlled me like my parents wanted it to, I didn't feel normal. I was put into a fake "happiness" that only lasted half a day until I took another pill. I understood my parents' intentions—my energy was too much for them and I could never control it. But the moment I put the pill in my mouth, I felt my real emotions change into false ones.

Just thinking about it makes the lump in my throat fully form.

I look out the window to see we are pulling into the parking lot of a big, white building.

We're finally here. Let's just get this over with so I can go home.

I let out a sigh and follow my parents to the door. My mom presses a small, red security button.

Why would a therapy place have this much security?

A woman lets us in and I sit in one of the chairs while my parents approach the person at the front desk. I'm used to waiting—we've been going to these appointments for years.

I think about why my parents started sending me to therapy: the constant anxiety that made me skip school in ninth grade. The pills had affected my friendships—they made me say things I didn't mean, and I was always up front in conflicts. But even before the pills affected me mentally and emotionally, they affected me physically. When I was prescribed Adderall, my friendships all went downhill, along with my physical being.

✧

"Ew. I can see your ribs."

"Oh my god, put your shirt down."

I was with my friend, Natalia, and her two friends who always put me down. We were all walking toward her house, which was a few blocks away from mine, when they commented on my ribs.

I stopped and stood alone in the middle of the street as they walked ahead, laughing, adjusting their bras and walking in a way they thought made their butts look good.

What was so funny about this? Because I wanted to be pretty and girly like I never could be?

When we got to Natalia's house, I heard one of the girls say to her, "I don't even know why you hang out with her. She's trying too hard to be like us."

The other girl joined in and said, "Have you seen how skinny she is?"

I was speechless. They continued talking, but I couldn't hear them because my ears were ringing. I zoned out, wanting my body to just evaporate.

Later, I went home and looked at myself in the mirror hanging on the back of my door—the one that had never before revealed to me what I truly looked like. The mirror that never seemed to showed how the clothes hung on my body like a coat hanger. I looked normal through my own eyes, and my parents had never made me aware of my weight problem, either. But as I ran my fingers down my body, I realized it didn't feel like a normal body should; I felt mostly bone and barely any meat.

Why is my body so ugly? I'll never be pretty like them. I wish I was.

My head spun and I felt like I was going to faint, but I didn't. I just stood there, like my soul had been ripped away.

My mirror had been photo-shopping me.

"Ew, put your shirt down" echoed in my head over and over. I squinted my eyes and looked closer in the mirror. I lifted my shirt and saw the outline of my ribs. I pulled my shirt back down and turned away. I didn't want to believe what was happening to me. I only wanted to fall asleep and forget everything.

✶

After a few minutes, a security guard motions me to follow him. I look at my parents and they stare back at me with worried expressions.

I follow him behind heavy, steel doors, noticing the faint smell of chemical cleaning products. The floor squeaks as I take slow, hesitant steps into the room. A woman wearing a business suit then walks me into a yellow room with a window looking out to the steel doors I just walked through. The surroundings seem off. It doesn't look like a therapy place. I wipe my sweating palms off on my pants as the woman starts talking. I tune her out and stare at the wall behind her, but I do hear one sentence come out of her mouth:

"You'll be here for 30 days or more."

Time stops and I can hear only my own breath. My heart rate increases rapidly.

"No, no, no. Wait. Hold on. So I can't leave? I can't even say goodbye to my parents?"

"No, you can't." She responds as if I should already know this.

Why would my parents do this to me?

I can barely comprehend her as she finishes talking because the wave from my nightmare is closing in.

Am I still asleep?

A Note from Kyana

After 46 days of rehab, I was happy to be free of pills and to let my body become clean of those fake feelings. While I was there I learned self-control and how to better evaluate things during the hard times. By the end, I had forgiven my parents for tricking me into rehab; all in all it was for the best and it really did help me. I finally had hope to be myself again: real feelings, real thoughts and a happier life. Moving to Scriber made everything much easier for me because I felt welcomed and was no longer ignored or forgotten by teachers. I have exceeded my goal of doing a lot better in school and will graduate in June. I am very proud of how far I've come and how I've pushed myself to do better. My future dream is to become a photographer and a writer.

A BLADE WON'T CUT IT

KENNETH ASH

Through my blurry vision I see the scissors in my right hand and the towel in my left. I stick my left arm out and cry more. Through my sobs and heavy breaths I snip the scissors in growing anticipation. The tears drop off my face and onto my arm. I cry, shake, and tighten my fists from the memory of the events that occurred earlier.

⚜

I was laughing and yelling along with my friends in the lunchroom like I usually did, even though I would have rather eaten alone. The smell of pizza and greasy fries filled my nostrils and the screams and yells from other students echoed off the walls. I was pretending to be happy so nobody would ask me why I wasn't talking and interacting; everyone else seemed truly happy with no acting. The bell rang to signal our fifteen minutes of free time.

I got up, put my tray away and walked out the double doors to the outside area. I saw my friend Jacob and tried to catch up to him. He had a lot of friends and was very popular. We were really close, the type of friends who could joke around about anything without being hurt. Being an only child, I had no brother to pal around with, so for him to treat me like a brother for the past six months was the best thing that had ever happened to me. But Jacob was standing next to Darin, who was always rude to me.

As soon as Darin saw me, he looked at Jacob and said, "Run!"

I watched the person I thought was my friend take off without even looking at me. My heart shattered.

I didn't know what else to do so I walked over to another group of friends I had known for a year. But as soon as I got there, they also ran away from me without saying a word. In that moment I felt like I had no friends.

I sat down against the wall and curled into a ball, covering myself with my jacket and shutting myself from the world. I heard laughing, so I poked my head out and saw a group of six or seven kids a few feet in front of me. Jacob was smiling and laughing, the sun shining off of his sunglasses, his blonde hair golden. My soccer teammate, Matthew, stood next to him. Matthew and I were never really close but I considered us to be somewhat friends. I watched as one of the kids took out a bag of baby carrots, opened it up, and threw one at me. It landed right at my feet. Covering my face again, I put my head back down and felt more carrots hitting me all over—my legs, my head, my shoulders. I clenched my teeth so hard I thought they would break and balled my fists so tightly they turned white. I picked one of the carrots up and threw it back. They didn't react. They just kept throwing and laughing.

I shut myself from the world again—this time more tightly. I heard a faint *thud* by my ear and saw a pinecone on the ground next to me. They had moved from carrots to pinecones. Peeking out from my sweatshirt, I watched as Matthew spit a piece of gum at me. It seemed to play in slow motion as it flew through the air and landed close to my left leg.

Finally the bell rang, ending what seemed like an hour of torture. As they left, they laughed as if nothing had happened and no one had been emotionally scarred for life. I stood up and found fifteen carrots, twenty pinecones and the piece of chewed gum surrounding me.

As I walked to class, someone yelled, "Stop thinking about your horrible life!"

*

I take the scissors and run them across my bare arm. Little drops of blood appear all along the cuts. The drops grow bigger and run down my arm. I press the towel against the cuts and the blood transfers from my arm to the cloth. I shake as I look at what I've just done and cry, remembering a time when Jacob was the only person at school who helped me. When he was the only one who cared.

*

When I entered the music room after school to practice my violin, Jacob was there playing his trombone. I saw him and my stomach filled with thousands of butterflies because I had worked up the courage all day to tell him something I had never told anyone. I felt like I was going to puke. I walked over to him and asked him to come with me to a back room. He nodded and followed me.

"Jacob, I have something important to tell you," I said.

"What is it?" he asked.

Even though I had met him only a month before, I felt like I could trust him with my biggest secret. I took a deep, shaky breath as I entered the land of no return. "I'm gay," I said. Speaking the words lifted the weight of the world off my shoulders. I eagerly waited for his response. I feared the worst.

"So? I don't care," he said. "That's who you are and I support you. Our friends will, too." He shrugged his shoulders like he didn't care, but his smile told me that he really did.

My shoulders relaxed, my breath stabilized and the fear cleared from my mind.

"Thank you for supporting me," I said, tears in my eyes. "You don't know how much it means to me." I thought everyone hated gays and treated us like shit all the time, so I was the happiest I had ever been. I grabbed him and pulled him in for a hug which he didn't fight. I kept thanking him and crying. I was so grateful to have such a supportive friend.

⁂

I drop the scissors and weep. As the blood drips onto my sheets I hear all the names and insults people have said over the years—the most used and the most hurtful: *Fag, Cock-Sucker, Waste of Time, Piece of Shit, Nobody likes you and nobody ever will, You don't have any friends.* I cry harder than I have in a long time. I feel all alone in the world.

The darkness surrounds me, slowly closing. I run but I'm not moving. I fight the ongoing battle with the little strength I have left, even though I have already lost.

"Where am I?" I shout, but I get no answer. "Who am I?"

All the people who have bullied me walk out of the shadows. *"You are all alone. No one will miss you and no one cares,"* they answer in unison.

I am lost, never to return. I sit alone in the dark wondering what will happen next. The darkness is depression. Depression is me.

A Note from Kenneth

After this happened in eighth grade I continued cutting for a year. It got so bad I went to the hospital for trying to kill myself. When I got out I made a vow to never cut again because I was not happy in the hospital and I didn't want to go back. This is a struggle I continue to fight as a ninth grader, but being at Scriber has helped me because I have people who care about me and understand where I'm coming from. When I came here I was sick and tired of hiding my true self, so I came out and everyone was supportive and nice about it. I decided to write this story so other people know that they're not alone in their struggles, and I want people who read this to never give up like I almost did. Now I dream of having a husband, kids and being a marine biologist/storm chaser. I have renewed strength and am currently winning my battle against depression. I am finally awake from the sleep that depression had put me in.

"This is my fight song. Take back my life song. Prove I'm all right song."
—Rachel Platten, "Fight Song"

CONTACT HIGH

MAKAYLA BOULET

My AP environmental science final is on the desk in front of me when I get the text. My matte black Starbucks cup is half empty next to it, the taste of Captain Morgan in my mouth. It was full an hour ago when I got to school—my first day here in two months. I knew when I woke up I needed to be numb to make it through the day, even though I only came to say goodbye to my friends before dropping out.

I look to my phone and read the message from my father. *Your secret isn't a secret anymore. You're a sinner and you will never live a fulfilling life being gay.*

Tears flood my eyes as I grab my cup, get up from the desk and hand my test to the teacher.

"Nice drawings," he says, smiling.

"Extra credit?" I manage.

"Good one," he says as he watches the familiar sight of me stumbling out of class. I never stay, especially when I'm mad. When I'm mad I need to pace.

Out in the hallway my mind races. I don't know what to feel. *How did he find out?* I think as I chase my thoughts with more rum. I just don't understand how he can judge me for something I can't control when I've never judged him for the things he could have controlled.

I think about the events that have happened since I lived with him in the sixth grade, when I was still innocent. Not long after that I got expelled, stayed home and smoked weed all day. The next year, a girl I met in the bathroom asked me to skip school and get high, and I said, "Yes." Soon after, that same girl and I stayed at a sketchy motel for a week straight and blew thousands of dollars of her insurance settlement on coke, molly, weed and alcohol.

All of these memories, along with the rum, are making me dizzy. The worst memories come up, too: waking at five in the morning on the sidewalk. Saying "no," when being drunk didn't really mean "no."

I hate my life. I'm ruined. I just want to get out.

I think about how it all started, a twelve year-old surrounded by so many drugs.

✦

My grandpa walked in the room, his ankle monitor flashing; he was on house arrest. He grabbed his weed pipe, or, as he called it his "special rock."

"Hey, Small Fry," he said as he crossed the room and opened the office door, quickly closing it behind him. Whenever someone opened that door, smoke rushed out and flooded the room.

I was eating chicken Top Ramen and watching *Family Guy* with my dog, a pit bull named Sally, while my grandpa, dad, and all of their friends went in and out of the office. They smoked weed, popped pills, snorted stuff and drank. Day after day.

I had been living with my dad and grandpa for four or five months. I moved there the summer after fifth grade—after my mom told me to pack up and get out. Before living with my mom, I lived with my dad and his wife, Alicia, until they divorced. I went from a loving, caring home with them—getting a lot of attention, maybe even too much—to living in homes where I got no attention at all. All I ever did when I came home from school was listen to everyone party in the office and sit in front of the TV.

Dino walked in. He lived on our futon in the living room. I always sat on the couch farthest away so I didn't have to smell the terrible odor coming from it. He had yellow teeth—a few were missing—ear length black hair, and a smile that could churn dairy. The stench of alcohol and weed covered him.

"Hi, MaKayla," he stuttered.

I quietly whispered, "Hi," before he disappeared into the back office.

My dad's car pulled into the driveway; he must have just gotten off work. He normally got home around six o'clock, unless he went to the bar first. I heard the car door slam shut. He walked in covered with paint from his house-painting job. He was scowling and his teeth were clenched tightly as he walked into the kitchen and grabbed a beer.

"'Sup, MaK?" he said in between chugs.

"Hey, Dad!" I said as I watched him make his way to join everyone else. I was always excited to see him; I craved his attention. But when he was home, he was always either in the back room or his bedroom. The only time I talked to him was when he occasionally dropped me off or picked me up from school. His girlfriend took me to school most of the time, and we always went to McDonald's.

I felt rejected, like nobody wanted me around.

Dino came back out of the office, walked into the kitchen, grabbed a piece of raw chicken, and started eating it.

"Raw meat? Really?" I cringed with disgust.

"Oh, it's okay. I'm native so it won't affect me," he said, then walked back into the office.

I hated the constant stream of people coming in and out. I wanted to die. I wanted my life back. I wanted to be with Alicia again—the person I considered to be my mom. I lost my whole family when she and my dad divorced. I didn't see the people I knew as siblings, cousins, aunts or grandparents because they were all on Alicia's side. She wanted me to stay, but I couldn't. I had to live with one of my parents.

I wanted to be anywhere but there. Sally, who was lying next to me with her paw on my shoulder, looked at me with complete love. I took her, my only friend, to my room to disappear.

※

As I walk in circles I start to laugh. I always laugh when I feel something painful because I don't know how to show emotion any other way. Whenever I talk about anything sad, I just laugh about it. When I'm uncomfortable, I laugh like crazy. If anyone saw me now, pacing and laughing, they would think I was crazy.

I need to calm down, I think to myself when I realize how drunk I am. I stumble my way to the library—where I've spent a lot of time working—and think about all that will go to waste when I drop out.

The room is spinning around me. Everything is a blurry haze.

My father hates me, I keep repeating in my mind.

As I chug the last third of the rum left in my cup, my eyes dart around the library. I see an empty table in the furthest corner. I walk over to it, fall into the chair and rip my hood over my head to escape the reality I am in right now.

I sink down, drift into my thoughts and fall asleep.

A Note from MaKayla

After this scene, my father and I went for about a month without talking, but we finally worked things out and have become closer. Even though he didn't accept me for who I am at first, he has come around to the idea that I am gay. Both of us had to awaken to each other's situations; I later learned that he was hurting even worse than I was during that period of his life. I decided to write this story to show that no matter how bad the past was, you can't let it dictate your future relationships with family. Getting this story out has helped me express my emotions, because I am not good at sharing how I feel on a deep level; it's more than just a story. Right now I am working a full-time job and have my own apartment. My goal is to graduate either this year or early next, but I'm still working on improving my attendance to make that happen. My future dream and goal in life is to just be truly happy with whatever I am doing.

STEPPING FROM OBLIVION

KELLY MAKAVELI

This hospital bed smells like homeless people. My Converse are still on my feet, bucket hat and sunglasses still on.

This is the last place I want to be. The breathalyzer tells me my blood alcohol content is .218, but all I want is another shot of cheap, bottom-shelf vodka chased down with some flat generic soda from the two liter I left open all night. The thought of being home standing in front of the sticky counter comforts me as I lay stiffly on the bed.

I know I'm dying. I haven't "pooped like a big girl" in six months. At least that's what my boss from the bowling alley calls it. I've been vomiting everything I try to drink or eat for about three months now. I have to take at least three "practice shots" to try and keep any vodka down. It hurts my throat to have such an acidic taste running down to my stomach all the time. I have to do it though, or else life becomes something I can't handle. The phenomenon of craving is something I cannot wrap my brain around. I know I'm putting poison in my body, but in order to keep sane I must keep doing it. I don't want to live drinking like this, but don't believe I'm capable of anything else. I'm in a constant cold sweat, resulting in showers more than three times a day just to keep the scent of vodka seeping from my pores to a minimum. My face is so swollen I look like a puffy blow fish, and I'm covered in cuts and bruises. I'm not sure where the bruises came from, but the cuts I know I gave myself – I just don't remember doing it. When I black out I try to kill myself. I black out on each night after work and occasionally before work. I black out on my days off. I've tried to kill myself many times.

Being here means I'm trying to live. I've never tried life; I've never given myself a chance. But I'm not convinced I have any chances left.

I decided about a week ago it would be a good idea to come here. I had called into work sick again. I was switching between the bathroom, my bed and the kitchen, vomiting, sleeping and drinking. I was simply existing to drink. The sweat was pouring out of me and my brain couldn't concentrate on anything besides holding down liquor long enough to ease my anxiety—the feeling that I wasn't at home in my own skin. I was getting endless text messages from my coworker; with each one I could clearly imagine his compassionate eyes as I explained to him my thoughts of suicide and my lack of hope that life could ever get better. He was sending me links to treatment centers and websites, directing me to people who could get me the help I needed. There was a moment when I finally had enough alcohol in my system to make the first phone call. It felt like I called a million phone numbers after that, telling each person on the other end my age and how much I was drinking, and hearing the sound of pity in each voice as my insurance was denied. Each time I heard, "Sorry we aren't able to help you," the death sentence weighed heavier on my heart.

I gave up on calling and went back to drinking. I couldn't get comfortable, even in bed; finding out there was no way to escape was devastating. However, within an hour a random number popped up on my phone and I picked it up. During the conversation, somehow I strung together enough drunken slurs to agree to come in the next week when they expected to have a bed open. I spent the rest of the week trembling in fear of the future and trying to consume enough liquor to keep me well.

And now I'm here.

There are four beds in this room. Mine is in the far back right corner, number 110-3. To my left there's an unmade bed and the night stand next to it has a family picture—the circular black and white ones that I've gotten every year at the fair. The people in the picture look like one big happy family. I want to cry out in pity for the sick bastard who believes that bullshit "happy family" thing could actually happen. Instead I turn my head and look at the woman in front of me. I've been trying to avoid looking at her since I walked in. She is wearing the infamous hospital socks and is hooked up to an oxygen tank. Her face sags like a bulldog. She half grunts, half smiles at me when she sees me staring.

Am I actually here right now? I decide to close my eyes for a minute because the room is spinning. I kick off my shoes but leave my sunglasses and hat on—I don't want anyone to see past them.

The gentle nurse walks in pulling a blood pressure cart with wheels. She uses it to scan our bracelets to see the last time we were dosed. She closes the curtain around the oxygen tank lady, as if that gives them any privacy. When she comes back through the curtain, she says, "Kelly, we can't give you any meds because you're almost three times the legal limit and you still haven't given us a urine sample."

I look over at the water cup and remember I am supposed to be drinking it. At least it has crunchy ice and not cubed ice. I can't think through what she has just said. I know she wants me to take action, but it takes me a few seconds to respond.

"I think I could probably pee now," I say, slurring. It takes all of my strength to lift myself off the hospital bed. I stumble across the cold tile floor in my Seattle skyline socks. I grab the cold door knob and push, but the door is much heavier than I expected. My weak arms can hardly open it.

"Leave the door cracked, please," she says, softly.

Oh yeah, like I'm going to fake a UA in detox, I think. My chest tightens as I hold myself back from saying something snarky. I wish this lady would let me go back to the unpleasant bed. I've never even taken a UA. I put down a protective seat cover and fall onto the toilet seat. I start to pee in the cup and realize I'm really terrible at it; pee gets all over my uneasy, shaking hand. I seal the cup and make sure to wipe it off as well as I can with my blurry vision. I hand the lady the warm cup and return to my bed as quickly as possible. I can't see straight enough to be vertical for that long.

"Okay, let's get you TB tested, your blood drawn and a shot of Thiamine," she says.

I want nothing to do with her needles. I figure this getting sober thing is going to be a bunch of stuff I don't want to do. I can hardly muster up a thought dated past the next five minutes. The idea of the future seems so distant and false, as if it isn't meant to happen. Doubt spreads thickly over my mind.

My entire body shakes, then stops.

"Relax," she says, but I haven't gotten a shot since the sixth grade. I close my eyes and wait for her to break the skin. She pokes me right on a scar I inflicted on myself. She looks up from my wrist but I avoid eye contact. She wants this for me—I just don't know if I want this for me. I'm pretty good at that whole avoiding eye contact thing. I can't stand the painful look of disappointment in people's eyes, so I don't bother looking anymore.

Some of my friends use needles, for heroin. They describe it as the worst thing they've ever done but the best feeling they've ever felt. I never thought I'd be able to push past the fear that keeps needles out of my arms, but the shot she just gave me didn't feel the way I always predicted it would. My heart fills with a new fear: not being afraid of needles means it will be one hundred times more difficult to stay sober after this week-long detox.

To get out of my own head I ask, "What can I do besides lay here?"

"You can go to the movie room or drink some coffee in the games and TV room."

The game room sounds better than movies. *I hate movies.* I can't focus that long. I leave my room, walk directly across the hall and take a seat at a round table which feels like it consumes the entire room. To my left is a man who looks as if he's dying. His brittle body sits on a chair pad protecting him from a broken ass bone or something. He's probably 70 but he's dressed like a teenager. He wears plaid pajama bottoms and a different style of plaid print sweatshirt. He is watching some weird redneck show about getting bullet splinters out of an eye. I glance over at the shelf full of games which look like they've been there for years. I make an educated guess that they are all missing half the pieces.

"Hey, do you want to play a game or something?" I ask.

He doesn't take his eyes off the TV. His upper lip stiffens as he calmly answers, "No."

I want to go home. I don't belong here. The intake nurse told me I'd be the youngest person here, but I had no clue this is where people come to die. I don't want to feel such a fire in my stomach when I am forced to interact with people, but I do. If I can distance myself far enough from everyone, I can drink the amount I need without being judged.

I wonder what my mother is doing right now. She's probably at home crying into a shot glass, finishing the rest of the half gallon I bought last night. She's probably heartbroken that her drinking buddy is throwing in the towel. When I told her I wanted to get help, she tried to convince me not to go. The memory causes me to tense up. I don't want to think about her.

Mom, I think I'm going to die like this, I had written her in a text.

Oh honey, don't worry. I'll clean the mold off the window sill when I get home tonight. You'll feel better in no time, she texted back.

I had immediately burst into tears; I knew deep within my heart that the alcohol had me in its grips and was killing me with each shot I had to take. She knew how much I was drinking and still wanted to believe it was the mold that was causing all of my health issues. She was always there when I woke up, holding a shot glass out for me. She knew it was the only thing that made me tick. I imagine not knowing her daughter any way besides drunk must kill her.

I wonder where my father is and I think about the last thing he said to me. "You know rehab is for quitters, right?"

He had teared up as he handed me $60 in exchange for weed. "Fuck off," I barked at him in response to his bad joke. His tears showed he was aware of the damage he had done. *He's probably smoking crack alone in a dark room now*, I think.

I never wanted this. I never asked to wake up in the morning desperately seeking a hero, only to find alcohol. I never wanted to be 18 in detox.

"Oh, hey look, new kid," a shaggy-haired guy says as he walks down the hallway past the small room. He comes back after a few seconds, takes the only open chair and tries to look past my hat and sunglasses. "What're you in here for?" he asks, as if it's jail. He sounds like he has a scheme brewing.

"Alcohol. You?" I ask reluctantly.

"You're drunk aren't you? You lucky little shit. As soon as I get out of here I'm chugging the fifth of Fireball in the trunk of my car. My stupid dad searched my car and found my heroin. Fucking asshole kept my stash for himself. He didn't find my liquor, though!" he says with pride, as if having alcohol waiting for him puts him ahead of me.

Kill me now. His overgrown facial hair makes me uncomfortable. I slouch in my chair. I am still having trouble carrying my body weight. I wish I could sleep this off.

A kid walks in wearing a blue North Face jacket and Abercrombie jeans sagged so low his entire ass shows.

"What's up, dude?" Caveman says in greeting, like he hasn't seen him in days.

There are four different types of people in this room, including me, and I hate all of us. I normally hate myself, but being classed with these guys makes me feel like the scum of the earth.

"What time is it?" a groggy voice asks from the hall.

"About two," Caveman replies.

The groggy-looking guy is a tan, tall, round man who looks like he just woke up. He has a single mole on his chin that I can't take my eyes off of. He is balding and looks very unhappy. His slippers drag across the floor like he is in pain. He beelines to the decaf coffee. Everything in here is sugar and caffeine free.

The old man folds his newspaper and slowly gets up out of the chair. He grabs his ass pad and walks out of the room like a three-legged dog. *Why does everyone drag their feet in this place?* The groggy man grabs his coffee and joins me at the table.

"I'm Gus. What's your name?" he asks.

"I'm Kelly."

"What're you in for?" He asks this as if he's asked hundreds of people already.

Why is everyone acting like this is jail?

"I'm an alcoholic."

Saying it feels normal, as if I had accepted it a long time ago. I've said it out loud before, but always to justify how much I was drinking. I had never spoken these words in a detox center, admitting defeat. It feels good to finally tell the truth, since my life has been made up of only lies.

He badgers me with more questions on how much I've been drinking, when I started, and how I ended up here.

"Listen to me. When they ask your pain level, you tell them like an eight or nine. Same with anxiety. You hear me?" he says quietly, leaning in real close to my face.

I nod, but I don't really understand what he's talking about. I look back at the other boys and see that they are sniffing the hand sanitizer.

"Dude, you know you can drink that shit if you mix it with water," Gus advises in a low voice.

"Dude, I'm gonna go jack one of the pill cups and then we're on for shots?!" says Caveman.

"Nah man, not me. I'm going sober. You know that, bro," Gus says, shaking his head slowly.

Should I ask to join them or join Gus and be a lame sober kid? I'm truly torn because every fiber of my being is telling me I should continue finding ways to escape myself. Gus is as slothy as I am, except he's been here longer so the alcohol is all out of his system. I decide I've got enough alcohol in my system to avoid the hand sanitizer for now.

Gus is popping popcorn when the boys return with pill cups. I have no clue how they got them off the nurse's cart.

"You have to mix it up real good. I watched this guy in jail try it and he threw up everywhere. Don't get yourself into trouble, man," Gus says.

Gus' eyes are low and bloodshot, desperate. They are knowledgeable, but I wonder if anything he knows will help him get sober. He sure seems to know tricks on how to survive detox, though, so he's exactly the person I need right now.

Caveman takes a plastic stir stick from the coffee area and stirs up his next high. "Is this good enough?"

"Dude, I don't know, try it," Gus replies.

Caveman looks at Saggy Pants, who has been stirring his for about the same amount of time, shrugs and raises the pill cup in the air.

"Let's party," they say simultaneously.

I don't understand what a party is any longer. My idea of a party is a half-gallon of vodka and headphones. I have a feeling their party is as over as mine is. A party is when getting loaded is still fun, and it hasn't been fun for me for a while. It's more of a chore, really.

The nurse walks in within seconds of them throwing out the empty makeshift shot glasses. She goes around and takes everyone's blood pressure. She comes to me last. "How's your pain level?"

Remembering what Gus told me, I reply, "I'd say like an eight."

"Anxiety level?"

My fear level is rising as my blood alcohol content falls. My security blanket is slowly melting, but I don't know how to properly communicate this. "I can't take this!" I shout. "I want to go home and drink. Why am I here?"

My new friends' eyes dart to me, startled by my outburst. That's the most I've said since I've been here. The starry-eyed look caused by drinking the hand sanitizer leaves their faces.

"Okay, we're going to get you some meds and some dinner," the nurse says, taking a step away from me.

She hands me a pill cup with five different pills in it—all different shapes and sizes. Seems like a good time to me. I take them all at the same time, hoping for a quick escape. I don't even think to ask what they are. *I knew Gus had my back.*

"Bro, she's a savage," Caveman says.

"How about you go take a nap now? It will get better," the nurse says.

"I'm not tired," I snap back.

It won't get better. How could she say it will get better? She has no clue. I'm fucked. I am literally going to die. I'm so unsatisfied with life and I'm ready for it to end.

She leaves and I lean in to Gus. "Is it weird?" I whisper, "I think I'm already feeling the meds she gave me. It's only been like five minutes."

"No, no you're not. Trust me. You'll know. That Librium is no joke," he whispers back.

It seems Gus and I only communicate quietly, like getting sober is a secret around here.

Gus goes on to tell me about his drinking. How he hides it, how much, and how it's hurt him. Since he's talking about drinking he speaks at a normal volume. Maybe it's only hope and survival that's spoken in secret. He's the only person I've ever met who drinks like me.

I get up without saying anything and head back to the room because I don't know how much longer I can keep my eyes open. The fifteen-foot walk feels like an eternity now that the alcohol is wearing off and the pills are kicking in.

The first thing I see is a red plate with a red dome on top. I lay in bed, pull the table up and pull off the lid.

You've got to be fucking kidding me. A hamburger. I haven't been able to eat anything in three months and this is not how I'm going to start. The meat is black and the bun looks like it's left over from last month's picnic. The scent of the leathery fries makes me gag.

I push the table away and let the pills take over my entire body. I feel light, as if the crippling weight of depression has been lifted. This is the feeling I chase, a constant frequency of nothingness. My soul feels fresh, as if no damage was ever done. It feels like I'm no longer Kelly, as if I get to just be my heart and lungs for a while.

I wake up, as if in a dream, to a nurse. "Kelly, I need to take your blood pressure."

Shaking, I find the strength to lift my arm.

She reads the numbers but I don't hear them. All I want from her is more meds.

"Here's a cup for water and here are *these*." She places the pill cup within my reach. I take them all at once, just like I did the first time.

I return to a sweet, drug-induced sleep. When I wake up the lady in the bed next to me is gone; her bed is made and there is no sign of her anywhere. The bulldog woman is gone, too. I'm all alone. I have no clue how long I slept. The only light I see is coming from the window on the door that seems so far away. Even though it's dim, I swear I can see people moving around, a bunch of them. I remember reading about this online: delirium tremens, caused by severe alcohol withdrawals. Hallucinations that normally last up to 48 hours, *if* you survive the seizures. I close my eyes and hope I never wake up. I hope I never have to face this addiction again. I hope it wins, because I know I won't. This is the bitter end. I don't want to fight it.

I feel a hand touching my shoulder, bringing me back again. "Kelly, we're going to take your blood pressure," Cindy says.

I'm pretty sure I've never seen this nurse and I don't think her name is Cindy. Although, something is telling me to call her that. I hate the nurses waking me up. It seems like it's every five minutes.

"So, what are your plans after this? Have you looked into treatment centers?" she asks as she takes the meds out of the little plastic wrappers.

"No, I have to leave and go back to work. I have a life you know," I say. I mean to speak with confidence, but it comes out rude. She's just trying to do her job and help me, and I am just trying to stick to my plan.

"I know. I just thought I'd bring you this so you can look into it, in case you change your mind." She sets the pamphlet down on the table next to me as if I will actually read it. I take my meds and then roll back over, falling deep into sleep.

When I open my eyes again there's no nurse, but there is someone sleeping in the crazy lady's bed. A big bouquet of flowers sits on the table next to her bed, as if she's been cast for the lead role in some sappy movie. She isn't covered by a blanket and she's wearing jeans. Even though I've been sweating more than I ever thought possible, I still keep my blanket on when I'm in bed. I decide I'm hungry so I find enough energy to lift my head, then my shoulders and each leg individually. I put on my bucket hat and sunglasses and scoot across the floor, still wearing the same clothes I came in with. I have no clue how long I have been in this place. When I make it into the game room I begin to pop popcorn and take a seat at the round table.

"Want to play a game?" I ask an old man who is also sitting at the table.

"No," he says.

I remember I asked him before. Where has my mind gone?

When my popcorn comes out of the microwave, it's steaming. It looks like the most amazing thing I have ever seen. I eat as much of it as I can, wash my hands and return to my room. I'm pretty sure the new girl is dead.

"No one wants to play games in this stupid place," I say out loud, to no one.

The dead girl springs up and says, "I'll play!"

I walk across the hall to the game room and I grab Battleship. I plop down on her bed and begin to pull out the pieces so we can begin. She sighs at the fact I chose Battleship, but she is still willing to play.

"Dammit, what drugs are they giving me? I feel stupid," I say.

"I'm not sure. I don't even take Ibuprofen, so trust me, I'm not liking the meds either. I'm going straight to treatment after this, so they better stop dosing me pretty soon."

She sounds certain that she can stay sober if she goes to treatment. Out of nowhere a foreign thought occurs to me.

Maybe I should go.

And then two familiar thoughts:

That's a stupid idea.

Sounds like a waste of money.

The nurse comes and puts me back to sleep again.

I wake up again, extra groggy. I have no clue what time or day it is. I have no clue what's real and what's fake or what I'm seeing. I get up to escape the dark room. I walk into the hallway and am immediately struck by the bright overhead lights, almost shrinking me to my knees. But I keep moving forward, ending up in a chair by the vending machines. Thankfully, I have my Hello Kitty notebook with me so I can write down what's happened so far, now that I've been stripped of every distraction and am left with nothing besides my brain and a pen.

An angry police officer walks briskly past me. He's looking for me. Why can't he see me? I'm sitting in plain sight. I become scared and hide my head in my knees. As I look up I realize it's another hallucination.

"Are you Kelly?" a male voice asks.

Still scared, I almost say no, but instead I burst out, "Yes, why?"

"I need to take your blood pressure. I'm the nighttime nurse. My name is Paul."

I extend my arm. I feel like I've done this a million times.

"It's getting a little better," he says.

I'm not sure how he knows that, since I've never met him before. It must mean his little blood pressure cart thing has some of my records on there.

"So, can you read me my liver results?" I dare to ask. I have nothing to lose at this point.

"Oh no, no. I'm not authorized to do that," he says, shaking his head uncomfortably.

"C'mon, please? It's late. No one will even know. Plus, it's my liver. I think I deserve to know," I beg.

He pauses, considering. "I suppose I could," he says slowly. He drops his shoulders, admitting defeat.

I'm surprised; that was much easier than I thought. I assumed he would hand me medication and tell me I needed rest. He stops what he's doing on the blood pressure cart and walks around to the other side of the counter, sits down and opens something up on his computer. Since I'm not allowed on that side I put my elbows up on the counter and wait for answers.

His jaw drops, his eyes get big and he slowly puts his hand over his mouth. The disbelief in the air wraps around us both like a thick smoke cloud.

"This can't be right. How much were you drinking?" he asks in a low tone, almost a whisper.

"I don't know. I buy a half gallon a day. I'm not sure what happens to it, though," I answer quietly.

"I've only seen one person as bad as this. She was a 45 year-old woman. She's dead now." He says this quickly, as if the words burn his lips on the way out.

"Tell me the numbers," I demand.

"272," he says.

"I don't know what that means."

"It means you can never have another drink again, if you want to live."

A Note from Kelly, 2013 graduate

I began writing this story in the detox center, carried my notebook with me throughout treatment, and started to type it when I got out. Writing has been a huge part of my life since I first published in Scriber's 2013 book *You've Got it All Wrong*, so I knew as soon as I stepped into detox, whatever happened next would be an experience I could use to help others in the same situation. I'm currently working on my own book, and "Stepping from Oblivion" is the first chapter. Waking up didn't come easy. The physical aspect you read about here was but a beginning; the real work started when I began to rebuild my life. The funny thing about waking up is looking back and realizing how asleep I really was. The closer I stay to consciousness, the closer I stay to happiness. Sobriety has been good to me. After detox I went to a treatment center in Kirkland, WA. When I left, I felt vulnerable, uncomfortable and alone. After an experimental phase of smoking weed after rehab, I found the spiritual solution I was looking for. At the time of this publication I have been sober from any mind or mood-altering substances for more than a year and a half. I am currently working with teenagers who have special needs and hope to one day further my education. No matter where you are or who you are, there is a solution for whatever is causing you to suffer. Wherever you are is a good place to start.

"If we wait until we're ready, we'll be waiting for the rest of our lives."
– Lemony Snicket

ACKNOWLEDGEMENTS

This student writing/publishing program would not be possible without the backing of the Edmonds School District. We are especially grateful for the support of Superintendent Nick Brossoit, Assistant Superintendent Patrick Murphy, and Scriber Principal Andrea Hillman.

We also want to thank the Hazel Miller Foundation, Apex/Bruce and Jolene McCaw Foundation, the Edmonds Kiwanis, and the Rotary Clubs of Edmonds, Lynnwood, and Mountlake Terrace for their continued support.

We are grateful for continued collaboration on storytelling projects with the Seattle Public Theater, the School of Life Project, and Edmonds Community College.

Finally, special thanks to Trudy Catterfeld for graciously guiding this year's production.

We appreciate all of you for helping to make this book possible.

Marjie Bowker has taught English and a little history somewhere in the world for the past 19 years: in China, Norway and Vietnam, in addition to her "regular" spot at Scriber. She is co-founder of The Scriber Lake Writing Program and is the author of *Creating a Success Culture: Transforming Our Schools One Question at a Time* and two curriculum guides: *They Absolutely Want to Write: Teaching the Heart and Soul of Narrative Writing* and *Hippie Boy Teaching Guide: Transforming Lives through Personal Storytelling.*

David Zwaschka has taught English over the last 25 years in Alaska, Tennessee, North Carolina and Washington, with moments of administration in between. His two years at Scriber have been a revelation; he has so enjoyed his work with this school's terrific students and dedicated staff. Dave enjoys running, reading, hiking in the North Cascades and not having any pets. He and his wife, Claire, have two daughters.

Books also published by the Scriber Lake High School Writing Program:

We Are Absolutely Not Okay, 2012, ISBN: 978-0-615-63860-7
You've Got it all Wrong, 2013, ISBN: 978-0-9894381-0-0
Behind Closed Doors: Stories from the Inside Out, 2014, ISBN: 978-0-9894381-1-7
We Hope You Rise Up, 2015, ISBN: 978-0-9894381-2-4

A word after a word
after a word is power.
Margaret Atwood

CPSIA information can be obtained
at www.ICGtesting.com
Printed in the USA
LVOW04s1519230616

493838LV00017B/521/P